LIKE A MIRACLE

Ernest C. Wilson

NITY BOOKS

Unity Village, Missouri

Contents

How This Book Got Its Name 5

My Watch Did Not Make Itself 9

What Is It that Says "I"? 25

By Taking Thought 39

But the Truth Is 55

What Shall We Do about Jesus? 67

The Many Sides of Man 81

You Asked for It 91

Your Faith Is Your Fortune 107

In Every Need, and in This 123

Adventures in Prosperity 135

"I Sat Where They Sat" 155

The Love of Law vs. the Law of Love 173

A Step Beyond 183

"Except Ye Become . . . " 195

How This Book Got Its Name

Of all the things that people tell me about the help they have found through applying the principles that this book is about, one of the most frequent and certainly the happiest of introductions is for them to say, "It seemed like a miracle!" That is the way they start to tell their story of something remarkable that has taken place in their life or in the life of someone close to them: a physical healing, the solution of some seemingly unsolvable problem, the attainment of some goal in life, the dissolving of some misunderstanding, the forgiveness of a wrongdoing, or an outcome that seemed "too good to be true."

These are the kinds of things, or people, or situations that you will find in this book.

The principles are true. The personal stories are true: they have actually happened to actual people. Many of them have happened to me. Some of them have been told about in articles I have written for *Unity, Weekly Unity,* and *Daily Word* magazines, in somewhat different form. Many of them would not be acceptable in a book of fiction because they seem too incredible, unless narrated by a writer more skillful than I.

What brings one person to the conviction that "man does not stand alone," that there is a supreme Presence and Power manifest in life, may not be what will bring someone else to a similar conviction.

You, personally, may not need to be brought to such

a conviction. You may already have attained to it, or can do as well without it. But if you feel the need of it, there will be a way by which you can find it. "Desire is prophetic of its own fulfillment."

Experiences that seem like miracles are apparently never identical to different individuals, yet there is an overall similarity that is reassuring. You will never find two identical leaves on a tree nor two identical snowflakes in a snowfall, yet there will be similarities that indicate a pattern or a law.

So when some seemingly far-out occurence comes into your life, it may seem like (and to all intents and purposes be) a miracle.

Through the pages of this book I want you to know

—A prayer that sustained a man through a crippling accident, and has brought countless others through challenges.

—A formula that prevented a suicide.

—The policies of a man who made a fortune of $7,000,000.

—The curious reason an attractive woman couldn't get a job where there's always a vacancy.

—A spectral voice that contradicted a young minister's firm conviction.

—The unorthodox way of finding the right doctor in an emergency.

—The incredible story of a last will and testament that no one in this world knew existed.

—How a modern Magdalene brought beauty to an Easter service.

—How ESP appears, mostly unrecognized, in everybody's life.

—A woman who "thought tall" and demonstrated it.

What these people did might not be the things for you to do. Methods conform to consciousness. But the prayers they used, and that others used, are universal in scope and application. And the successful outcomes of many challenges recounted here are basically the stories of human faith, prayer, courage, and overcoming, outworking in ways that are peculiar to each individual as your name, your personality, your idiosyncrasies are peculiar to you. You can do all things needful if you know and use the God-given power that is in you.

Some of the people whose stories illustrate the action of God in their life are world-famous. Some of them are from very humble walks of life. If one of them were telling you his story in person he would very probably begin with the words, "It seems to me like a miracle!"

It does to me, too.

My Watch Did Not Make Itself

How can a man believe in God when there is so much evil and greed and violence in the world?

How can he *not* believe in God when there is so much courage, heroism, unselfishness, love, and beauty in the world?

Neither attitude is satisfying to most persons—one or the other may merely serve to support an already established opinion. For belief in God is a very personal thing. I think you have to experience it rather than admit or deny it by logic.

One scientist, Dr. A. Cressy Morrison, declares: "By unwavering mathematical law we can prove that our universe was designed and executed by a great engineering intelligence.

"Suppose you put ten pennies, marked from one to ten, into your pocket and give them a good shuffle. Now try to take them out in sequence from one to ten, putting back the coins each time and shaking them all again. Mathematically we know that your chance of first drawing number one is one to ten; of drawing one and two in succession, one in one hundred; of drawing one, two, and three in succession, one in a thousand, and so on; your chance of drawing them all, from number one to number ten in succession, would reach the unbelievable figure of one chance in ten billion.

"By the same reasoning, so many exacting conditions are necessary for life on the earth that they could not possibly exist in proper relationship by chance."

Another, Dr. Warren Weaver, writes about his resolving of the apparent conflict between science and religion. He says in part: "Every new discovery of science is a further revelation of the order that God has built into His universe.

"How does my belief square with my respect for and confidence in science? And what kind of God do I believe in?

"A table, viewed with the precise tools of the atomic scientist, is a shadowy, swirling set of vague and elusive electric charges. So viewed, the table completely loses its large-scale illusion of solidity.

"Now, no scientist has ever seen an electron. 'Electron' is simply the name for a consistent set of things that happen in certain circumstances. For a while, physicists thought that the electron was a particle. Then they recognized that electrons are wave motions. Today they think of electrons as being both (or either) particles and waves. Yet nothing seems to them more 'real.'

"As for the second question: On the emotional level, my relationship to God is a highly personal affair. . . . When I am trying to work out within myself a problem of right or wrong, then God is a clear and unambiguous voice, an unfailing source of moral guidance. I cannot think of a single instance in my life when I asked what was the *right* thing to do and the answer was not forthcoming."

The Right Thing

With him, I can attest to the efficacy of this method. I "came upon" it one time when I was faced by the strongly voiced opposition to some of my views by another (and very articulate) minister.

How can I pray about this? I asked myself.

I could not honestly pray "for" him or "against" him. Finally the "revelation" came to me that I could pray, *"All things conform to the right thing, under grace and perfect law."* Incidentally, or maybe consequently, the whole disagreement sort of vanished into thin air and was never heard of again!

Before we leave the conclusions of scientists about God, let it be said that some scientists declare themselves to be atheists or at least agnostics. I have never had an opportunity to talk with one of these, but among laymen I know who assert similar views, I have frequently had the feeling that they were almost imploring me to convince them otherwise.

As Dr. Warren Weaver says, "On the emotional level, my relationship to God is a highly personal affair."

It is less a matter of thinking, of reasoning and logic, than it is of feeling; feeling that on occasion takes a very emphatic form.

For instance: My first assignment as minister "on my own" was to a small congregation in a large church in Galveston, Texas. It was a rugged experience in the beginning. I was not yet twenty-one, a very callow youth. But people rallied round. There were lots of children, and I loved working with them. Attendance increased. The church prospered. One day I had a strong urge to go into the sanctuary all by myself and have a service of gratitude to God for my many blessings.

A Mystic Voice

I went to the little reed organ and played a simple

11

prelude and a hymn; to the lectern for a Scriptural reading; and to the pulpit for a spoken prayer. Like "Merton of the Movies" who knelt by his cot back of the store in which he worked, and prayed, *"O God, make me a good actor!"* I found myself praying, *"O God, make me a good minister!"* I gave thanks for the increasing attendance, the rewarding financial prospects, the seemingly transformed lives of some of the people, and I thought, with a kind of youthful complacency—or youthful pride—that I would probably be there for many years to come, when I heard a voice speaking into my right ear, declaring "You won't be here very long!" I was shaken, incredulous. I *could not* have imagined it. Yet I *must* have imagined it. The voice was as clear, as real, as strong, as any heard in normal conversation.

Call it imagination, call it the subconscious, call it what you will, it was the first of numerous related other-worldly experiences that I have had through the years, which have convinced me that there is a higher Power—a Power that at times mercifully, at times sternly, sometimes gently, makes Itself known to bumbling humanity.

That it was in that early instance a presage of things to come was soon evident.

The church in which I served was a very old building. It had been inundated by two disastrous floods. Water had reached a height of four feet in the ground-level assembly room. Plaster had been replaced by willing but amateur workmen, where the laths and uprights of the walls had been exposed. The new plaster continually yielded a faint but appreciable sifting of white powder around the edges of the room. I was never quite content with the services of the volunteer janitor, and after his departure for the day, would often man his wide push-broom and sweep, sweep, sweep the ancient floorboards. But no matter how many times I would do so, I never seemed to be able to get *all* the silt out of the boards.

A Crisis

A month after my disembodied-voice experience I suddenly became ill.

There was an epidemic of flu.

I had rehearsed some seventy children in a Christmas play.

My mother had come from Montana to visit me over the holidays. I took her to a matinee movie. In the midst of it I had an all-gone feeling that moved me to say: "Mother, I'm going to be ill. Let's return to the church."

I lay down on a daybed in my study, half-delirious.

I felt I must have medical help. I might have exposed seventy children to "something." "Do you know a physician in whom you have confidence?" Mother asked me. I shook my head.

"What shall we do?"

I worded an audible prayer that went something like this: *"Dear Father God, I am here only by Your grace, here to serve You and the people of this congregation. I don't know what has happened to me. I don't know much about being sick. I know that You know all about me. I am turning to You for help. I trust You to guide and direct me to the human channels of your appointing. Please make Your guidance very clear and plain, because my senses seem blurred and I do not know what to do. I praise and give thanks for all Your many blessings to me along the way that have brought me to this present place, this present time. I give thanks that even now You are making way for me to find the help I need. In Jesus' name, Amen."*

"Now what?" my mother asked. It seemed like someone else talking when I said: "Get the phone book. Turn to the yellow pages, to physicians. We'll have another prayer—a silent one—and God will tell us whom to call."

We did so, and she started reading the names, with pauses in between, and I kept shaking my head. Finally she got clear down into the S's, and came to the name Starky. "That's the one. Send for him." I said.

She did, and he proved to be a fine and kindly physician. The diagnosis was scarlet fever. "There are two alternatives: send you to the pest house, or quarantine the church and let your mother care for you in it."

Of course we chose the latter, and instead of the six or seven weeks anticipated, it was only twenty-nine days before the quarantine was lifted, and we went to a hotel to stay while the church edifice was being fumigated.

Conviction of Guidance

"On principle" I had believed in the presence and power of God. These Galveston experiences fortified my belief. There was

—the disembodied voice

—its message, "You won't be here long"

—the illness, supposedly contracted from the dust of the many sweepings

14

   —the guidance to a fine and kindly physician

   —the swift recovery,

And finally, the fulfillment of the prediction, "You won't be here long."

And Later

There was the summer when I spent some months in Los Angeles and was returning home to the congregation I served in San Diego. A dinner was planned to welcome me. In those days it was a long trip, five hours of slow driving, often between the same two cars most of the way. This time it was an eventful trip. Let me quote from a letter I wrote to a Los Angeles friend the next day: "I hadn't gone a fifth of the way when I discovered that the engine was overheating, the radiator steaming. I stopped and found that the fan belt was broken. The nearest garage could not supply another belt. They would send to another garage for one. An hour passed before I was on my way again.

"Soon I was following the shore line southward. As I hurried to make time, the breeze from my car quickened that which came from the ocean. It was a warm day. I had thrown my coat on the back seat of my open touring car. The wind whipped my coat open; I felt some papers brush my cheek, and saw them sail blithely out over a wide expanse of soggy marsh."

Clutching at my coat, I discovered that two checks given to me that morning were missing. And then, as if that were not enough, a third incident of far greater moment took place. I had covered most of my journey, with only eighteen miles or so to go, when . . . But let me quote again from the letter:

"I made the Torrey Pines grade nicely, and was hustling along between it and La Jolla, approaching the Biological Grade . . . when I heard a peculiar grating sound near the right front wheel of the car, and stopped to see what was wrong. Would you believe it, the hub cap of the wheel and some of the ball bearings were gone! I had been coming heaven only knows how far— up the Torrey Pines grade at any rate—with nothing to hold the wheel in place!

"It was after five o'clock on a Sunday afternoon. I was between the two steepest and most winding grades in Southern California.

"I first tried hailing a car and sending word to some garage man to come and tow me in to La Jolla; but the cars I hailed whizzed merrily by. So I decided that the Lord must have been taking care of me for a good many miles, since the wheel had not come off (the tire had wobbled so much that the rubber was worn clear down to the fabric in spots), and that if He wanted me to write some more books, I should not topple off the Biological Grade with Henry (pet name for the car). Besides, it was then so late that any further delay would make me late for dinner—and what is an honorary dinner without the guest of honor?

"So I pushed the wheel on as far as I could, climbed back into Henry gingerly, said a prayer, and drove the remaining miles to the grade; then down the steep, winding road, with the wobbly wheel grinding and shaking away within a few inches of the shortest distance between me and sea level. Of course, I made it all right, and drove into La Jolla. As I passed the Thrifts' place the Lord was surely right alongside, for there in her chummy roadster sat Mrs. Thrift, just back from

16

town and preparing to put her car away. Fortunately for me, she had parked at the curb instead of driving into the garage. I should not have expected the Thrifts to be at home if I had not seen her. I told her what had happened, and we hustled Henry to a garage."

She and her husband got me into town in record time, with many exclamations over my foolhardiness in driving down the grade under the circumstances. The garage man confirmed their opinion next day. "Little short of a miracle," to quote again from the letter, "that I had made the grade or even gotten to it . . . He said that I had had one chance in a thousand. I didn't tell him about my arrangement with the Lord."

As It Truly Was

People say that we tend to magnify the dramatic side of unusual experiences, as we retell them through the years. So I'm glad I could quote from a personal letter written just a day after my driving hazard. And I find that in the account of the disembodied voice, and the way a doctor was chosen, what I have written here is almost word for word what I wrote of the experience many years ago. (I recalled that it had been published, and fortunately was able to find a copy of the publication and check with what I've just written.)

"When I am trying to work out within myself a problem of right and wrong, then God is a clear and unambiguous voice, an unfailing source of moral guidance. I cannot think of a single instance in my life when I asked what was the right thing to do and the answer was not forthcoming."

The words in the preceding paragraph are my sentiments, but are from the writings of the mathematician and scientist, Dr. Weaver, previously quoted, and published in Reader's Digest under the title, "Can a Scientist Believe in God?" Indeed, must not a scientist believe in God, whether by that name, or as Mind, infinite Intelligence, the Creative Principle of Being, or even as the Unknown?

More than Mind

The scientific approach to the mystery of life appeals to my mind. My thought reverts to the illustration of the ten pennies, and the mathematical chances against their appearing in the successive order prescribed. It justifies the feeling within me that what we call God may not be only the Mind of the universe but also the Heart. I think of instances in which it seems that Something greater than my own conscious knowledge or understanding has reached into my experience in time of need, as when through prayer I picked a doctor's name out of the yellow pages, and as before that in a time of worship a Voice spoke in my ear. I must accept—and gratefully—their comfort and encouragement, that leads me to say with the Psalmist, "Bless the Lord, O my soul, and forget not all his benefits."

Probably God, the Creative Principle of Being, is both Mind and Heart; and whichever leads us as individuals into a consciousness of His abiding presence is valid. To be "all heart" or "all mind" in the way that we use the terms seems undesirable. *"A soft heart, a sane mind, a sound body"* expresses better balance. Nevertheless, as individuals we tend to slant a little one way or the other, at least as pertaining to thought and feeling. In self-evaluation we tend to believe that we ourselves are pretty well balanced; it is those about us whose views are biased!

A Heart Doctrine

In the Christian ethos, it appears to this writer that the message of Jesus was essentially a heart doctrine (persons who lean toward the mental-intellectual view of Truth veer away from Jesus as a person and stress Christ as principle) and that of Paul was essentially mental and analytical. Neither was of course wholly the one or the other. Some modern teachers see Jesus as a great psychologist, far in advance of the times in which He lived. Yet at the same time He was a master of compassion, as we have noted elsewhere in this volume and others. And Paul, though noted for his intellectual nature and consequent appeal to scholars who like to consider everything without emotion, nevertheless balanced this nature by one of the most beautiful portrayals of the love-nature in literature: the thirteenth chapter of his first letter to the church at Corinth.

"God is Principle, God is Divine Mind, God is infinite Intelligence," as we have written elsewhere (in *Soul Power*). "But when we are in trouble, when we are lonely, when we feel inadequate to cope with the problems that seem so real to us, we feel the need of a personal God, a God who is interested in and responsive to our particular needs and longings."

"Get wisdom, and whatever you get, get insight," Solomon admonished long ago, but as a modern one-time king has said, "the heart too has its reasons," and mind without heart can be pretty cold and unfeeling, just as heart without mind can be maudlin. The intellect must be served, but it is feeling that brings about practical results in everyday living, that makes what people call "demonstrations" over difficulties.

So remember that God, who is the heart of the universe, is never more than a thought away. "The Lord is near to all who call upon him," the Psalmist assures us, and "The kingdom of God is in the midst of you," Jesus proclaimed. "Closer is He than breathing, nearer than hands and feet," the poet sings.

Wherever you are, you can reach God. Wherever you are, God can reach you.

God's love, His power, His help, His resources are ever available to you. He does not reject you, or condemn you, or fail you, or forsake you because of anything you have done or failed to do.

Who Moved Away?

You may have rejected Him for any one of a number of reasons. You may have felt guilty about some sin of omission or commission and not wanted to face Him. You may have feared His condemnation. You may have been disappointed in some experience in which your prayers were not answered (at least not in a form that you could recognize or accept). You may have decided that "there is no God," which usually means that you have not been able to accept some concept of God that has been presented to you.

Open your mind and heart to Him, especially your heart, for in spiritual things the heart is wiser than the mind. Let the feeling of His presence well up in you. God is the divine corrective. Whenever you consciously bring God into your life and affairs, things improve, get brighter, like the sun piercing through clouds, and dissolving them as well.

Are we not, then, punished for our mistakes, our shortcomings? No, not for them, but by them. In deepest truth the word *punishment* does not apply. Rather we are consciously or unconsciously choosing results. Everything we do or fail to do conditions its own response. What we send out tends to come back to us, increased and multiplied, like an echo. Action calls for reaction. Cause and effect are root and branch of the same tree.

The result of turning away from sunlight is to be in shadow, perhaps in darkness. If light is desirable to us, we may think of the relative darkness as being a punishment. Actually it is a natural result. (When the Psalmist sang of abiding "in the shadow of the Almighty," he sang as one who, accustomed to the hot and glaring sun of open desert, found shadow to be a refreshment and rest. Perhaps too he thought of his nearness to God, for in man's thinking, nothing can be much closer to him than his shadow.)

A Way to Go

Being in darkness and not liking it, we do not merely *wish* to be in the light. We take steps toward the light. The effort we make is an effectual prayer. Turning from darkness, we are "rewarded" by an access of light, as we were "punished" previously.

The sun does not withhold its rays from us because previously we have been in darkness. It passes no judgment. It shines on all who come within its radiance. In the very moment of your turning, the light blesses you.

You are "forgiven" for having been in darkness, in the very act of turning to the light. You are "for-given" because you have "given-for." You have given up the less desirable for the more desirable. And that is what forgiveness really means. Forgiveness is not a notion. It is an action.

Reward and punishment are variable terms. The punishment of mistaken action or inaction, mistaken notions and attitudes, is in having to live for a time in the consequences they have invited. But you may find these rewarding too, because in the process you learn and grow: like Holmes' "Chambered Nautilus," you build more stately mansions, and thereby find new levels of awareness, wider horizons of freedom.

When we are able to say, "I know better," we have taken the first step in overcoming a mistake or shortcoming. The next step is to do better. "If you know these things, blessed are you if you do them," said the great Teacher.

A youthful preacher was conducting an evangelical meeting, exhorting the congregation to repent of their sins and to accept Jesus Christ as their personal savior. He was interrupted by a cry, "Stop!" A young man, grimy and disheveled, with matted hair and dirty clothing, rose and challenged him. "How can you and your Savior help us? It is two thousand years since Jesus Christ came to teach us how to live, and there is still widespread war in the world, there is rape and murder and every kind of crime!"

The preacher seemed stunned by this attack. A murmur in the crowd subsided into silence. The disheveled youth was still standing. Finally the preacher broke the tension. "You are right," he responded, "Soap and water have been in the world for thousands of years, too, but they are no good to you unless you apply them."

A Progression

We grow by the truth we know and the use we make of it. There is a common saying that a child must fall down many times in order to learn to walk. It is the getting up and going on that is important.

So the growing soul neither deplores nor glorifies mistakes. He looks upon his life, and the life of others, as a progression. He gives thanks

—that he does not walk alone,

—that he is adequate and more than adequate for any challenge that comes to him from within or without,

—that God is a very present, immediate and available help,

—that with Him all good is possible, and only the good is enduringly true,

—that he can do all things needful for his life's fulfillment,

—that God's will for him is good, and

—that what God wills He also fulfills.

We do not all march to the same drummer. We cannot all reach heavenly goals by the same path. But be on some path that takes you "up higher." And don't wait until you know all the answers before you start applying what you do know, or you will wait a very long time. Splitting metaphysical hairs over the nature of God and Truth is, like consistency, "the hobgoblin of little minds." Do not be alarmed by the loud voices of those who use the intelligence God gave them to deny His existence. Out of World War II there came the saying, "There are no atheists in foxholes," which is a

23

way of saying that when mundane resources fail, every man instinctively appeals to some higher Power.

A higher Power than man created him, whether in six days or in six aeons of time (or more likely in the timeless realm of mind), and put him in a world of limitless possibilities that stagger comprehension.

I look at my watch. It reminds me of other commitments; reminds me, too, that "my watch did not make itself."

What Is It that Says "I"?

What is it that says "I"? It is that in you that makes you an individual. "I" is your unpronounceable name; that is, the name that no one else ever calls you. You never call anyone else "I." No one else ever calls you "I." It is your I-dentity, the self that is never ill, never defeated, never afraid, never unhappy, never bound or limited by circumstances. So we should not link it with any form of limitation; only with apology say "I am sick," or "I am afraid," or "I cannot succeed." Even the letter *I* is a kind of pictograph, the simplest portrayal of man as God's one creature that stands forth upright, to assert his oneness with his creator; the self you invoke every time you use the pronoun "I."

You involuntarily recognize this self when in the midst of some challenging opportunity or difficulty, you have a feeling that you are like an actor playing a part in a drama. You are greater than the part you play. The curtain will come down on this scene and rise on another, but you yourself are above the sway of what seems good and evil. *You are.* You testify to this when you simply say, "I am." Jesus testified to it when He said, "Before Abraham was, I am"; and when God instructed Moses to return to Egypt and lead his people out of bondage, Moses asked who he should say had sent him. The answer was: "Say this to the people of Israel, 'I AM has sent me to you.' "

In the name and in the nature of your true, change-less, abiding spiritual nature, you are undefeatable. In the temporal world, this does not seem to be so. We are in a world of duality, and constantly have to adjust to this fact! We can learn to do so with such understanding that we are not overwhelmed by it, but find dominion.

Our Dual Nature

Each of us appears as two persons in one. There is the not-too-impressive self whose image we see in the mirror: the self whose voice doesn't reach very far, who is none too sure of himself, who tends to depreciate his own abilities—and often overcompensates by a show of bravado.

Then there is the higher Self that is invisible but very real: the Self that silently says, "Don't be discouraged. Try again. You can do better"; the Self that demands of us more than we humanly think we can do; the Self that goads and coaxes and instructs and inspires us "to dream the impossible dream, to fight the unbeatable foe."

Jacob knew about this long before "The Man from La Mancha." The angel with whom Jacob wrestled, and to whom he cried out, "I will not let you go, unless you bless me," was that higher Self.

A couple whom I know and love have come through a soul-shaking experience that illustrates this duality. They have reared a fine family, have attained distinction in their community, found a kind of inward security that cannot be measured by their considerable worldly possessions.

Few of their friends know how close to being shattered were all these possibilities during and following World War II. The husband went through wartime experiences that seemed to violate many of the standards that were so characteristic of him. His special skills involved special privileges, and with them special temptations. He became involved in ways that threatened not only his future but that of his wife and family.

He returned home outwardly the same, inwardly a different man; cynical, bitter, lashing out at those who loved him most. It was only with the greatest effort on the part of his family and friends that a semblance of normal life was preserved.

The turning point came almost two years later. I had joined the family for some special occasion when the old self, more nearly the real self, of my friend began to emerge. The tense, strained look on his face had given way to calm, and he was tossing a ball back and forth with the children. I looked across the patio to where his wife was sitting. There was a glint of moisture in her eyes but a smile on her lips.

More Like He Is

"He's more like he is than he was," I said softly. She nodded.

Few of us, fortunately, go through such a traumatic experience as this friend of mine, but in one way or another we are each involved in the process of becoming more like what we truly are in our real self than what we have been expressing on the mundane level.

Transiently we are sons of earth, and the dust of Adam is still upon us. The capital *I* is obscured by the little one with the dot over it. But eternally we are sons of God and heaven. There are times when we seem to have lost our way. Maybe some of us feel that we have never known our way. But we are in the process of becoming in fact what we have always been in Truth.

Like Adam and Eve leaving the garden, like the Israelites leaving the Land of Darkness and wandering in the wilderness, or like the youth Jesus tells about who demanded his inheritance from his loving father and went out into a far country, we have incarnated in this mortal plane of life to discover—or perhaps to re-discover—who and what we are; to release the divine potential; to dream great dreams and make the dreams come true.

When we observe someone making progress in this great emprise, we may well say of him, "He is more like he is than he was."

One of the most graphic stories of this sort that I know is about an orphan boy who grew up in the slums of London. He worked his way through school. At times he slept in an empty packing box on the wharf. He had no "background," only a strong body, a keen mind, and "that something" within him that would not beg or whine, but kept urging him to try, to learn, to improve, to earn a better way of life. There were so many counts against him that he never dared to admit his doubts and fears. So whenever he was asked to do something that seemed beyond him he would attempt it, and mostly succeed.

People came to have confidence in him. Here was a young man who could be depended on.

"Someday," he thought to himself, "they'll find out that I'm a coward, that my self-confidence is a bluff, that I only agree to do things I'm asked to do because I'm afraid to admit I can't."

But they didn't. "I'll act as if I'm strong, I'll act as if I'm not afraid. I'll pretend to background and breeding, and maybe some of it'll sink in," he said to himself.

The Man Who Pretended

So he came to be known as a Successful Young Man. He was elected to Parliament, and one day was keeping a luncheon date with some of his peers at an exclusive London club.

He mounted the stairs to a great salon that stretched dimly before him. In the subdued light he could see men conversing in little groups here and there. Seeking his host, his glance reached down the length of the room, and he saw coming toward him a man whose stride and bearing suggested to him all the things he himself aspired to be.

"How I'd like to be like him!" he thought. And as he strode forward he found that he was looking at his own reflection in a mirrored wall.

He had become the man he had pretended to be.

In his pretense, our young Englishman was nearer the truth about himself than in what appeared to be true of him. His story is one of the oldest stories in the world, forever made new in individual experience. Joel is telling it in essence when he admonishes, "Let the weak say, 'I am a warrior,' " and Job brings us a similar injunction: "When they cast thee down, thou shalt say, There is lifting up" (A.V.).

Jesus assures us, "I do nothing on my own authority but speak thus as the Father taught me." Paul declares "I can do all things in him who strengthens me."

Shakespeare has Hamlet pleading with the Queen, "Assume a virtue, if you have it not." Emerson tells us, "A man should learn to detect and watch that gleam of light which flashes across his mind from within, more

important for us to be here than in the next world.

There is a purpose in life for each of us, though often we are not consciously aware of what it is, even while we are in the process of fulfilling it. When we feel thus confused it is helpful to pray about it, something to this effect: *"Dear Father God, I give thanks that divine order is Your law of the universe, and that my own life is a part of that divine order. I give thanks that You are with me, and will be to the ultimate fulfillment of being. Make Your guidance and direction very clear and plain to me. Instruct me where I need instruction, correct me where I need correction, but withal hold me steadfastly in Your matchless love."*

It helps too if we can take the attitude that we are where we are because, at least for the time, this is the place where we should be; that there is some service to render, some challenge to be met, some blessing to be found; that when the purpose for which we are here is served, either the situation will change, or we will, or both. Affirm prayerfully: *"I am in the right place at the right time, doing the right thing in the right way. I have faith in God, faith in myself, faith in my fellow men. I am God's child, and He is mindful of His own."*

As a minister I am often called upon to counsel with persons who ask the question, "Why am I here?" Among them are

—those who are onlookers at life and take little part in outward activities,

—those who are disappointed in love and declare they will never let that happen to them again,

—those who have not attained to some coveted goal in life,

—those who have shut themselves away from life.

Onlookers

Let us consider the onlookers. Their name is legion. Some commentators say we are virtually a nation of spectators. We pay an admission fee to watch others having a good time in competitive sports, or in ice shows or plays or movies or church. In these pursuits we have at least minimal contact with our kind; but for some, even this is too much effort, and refuge is taken in reading, or as a captive audience to that little-window-on-the-world we call television.

Performers, entertainers, teachers, ministers all are aware of this lethargy that appears to overwhelm many persons, and they seek to involve their listeners and/or viewers by inviting participation in theaters—in-the-round, "happenings," quizzes, workshops, panel discussions. If we expose ourselves to these we are likely to find them rewarding, more than worth the effort. We become like the man who attended a fraternal meeting each week. Upon returning home his wife would ask, "Well, dear, how was the meeting tonight?" Usually he would shrug his shoulders and answer, "Oh, it was all right, I guess."

Then one evening in response to her query, his answer was different. "Fine! I took part tonight."

Involvement

There is something about "taking part" along with others that brings a rewarding sense of fulfillment. Yet the joy of such participation is often denied or rejected by those who would be most blessed by it: the wallflower who would actually like to be in the swing of things, yet holds back, expecting others to make all the advances of fellowship; or the person who attends church services and at the close, confronts me with the complaint, "I've attended this church for months and not a soul has spoken to me." I'm tempted to respond (and sometimes do) with the question, "How many persons have *you* spoken to?" The answer usually is, "Well, it's their place to speak first."

On the other hand I think of one family—father, mother, and child—who made it a practice to drive over five hundred miles, two or three times a year, to attend our Unity services. Before they had gotten to the top of the wide steps leading into the church, they would have stopped to offer to snap a camera for some group of sightseeing visitors, or would offer a hand to someone who was negotiating the ascent cautiously, or to all and sundry just offer a wide grin of happiness in being among such altogether likable people in such an altogether delightful place.

People mostly want to be friendly. They want to be recognized as individuals, not simply as part of a crowd. One of the great charms of Jesus was that He always seemed to find time for the individual and his needs. He had a charismatic quality that others seemed subconsciously to recognize, that assured them they would suffer no rebuff. Sometimes it helps us in trying to radiate a similar spirit by praying in the words of an old hymn, "Gracious Spirit, dwell in me, I myself would gracious be," or more prosaically, to affirm: *The best in me greets the best in you. I like you.*

What about the people who are disappointed in love? I often listen to what people describe as "love problems." Usually I think this term is a misnomer. Our problems are not so much because of love, whatever form it takes—love of a person or many persons, or even love of an ideal or a cause or a career. It is not love that causes us suffering, but what we do in the name of love, or the various emotions we indulge that are really counterfeits of love: possessiveness, dictatorial attitudes, vanity, aggressiveness, or simply wanting to be loved.

To be truly loving always blesses us. To be truly loving blesses those whom and that which we love. What we demand in return may hurt us and hurt others, too. For the returns of love are not for us to dictate or command. They can only come to us by divine right. So say and try to mean it with all your heart as well as with your mind: *"I love as I would be loved, unselfishly, impersonally, in the spirit of Christ. Nothing and no one can keep from me what God has for me, and I neither need nor want anything else. 'I stand amid the eternal ways, and what is mine shall know my face.' "*

Instead of asserting, "I will never love anybody or anything again," the psychologically right response is, "I will love everything and everybody more, but I will not try to dictate results."

What of someone who has tried and failed to reach a cherished goal, and therefore abandoned all effort?

Blessings in Advance

His loss is not so much failure to reach the goal, as failure to discover that many of the greatest joys and blessings we experience are in being "on the way" toward a goal, rather than in the attainment itself. Besides, "A man's reach should exceed his grasp, or what's a heaven for?" Columbus failed to reach India but he found a new world. Madame Curie found radium when she was seeking something entirely different. Goodyear discovered the process of vulcanizing rubber through what seemed only an act of carelessness. A man stubs his toe on a rock and finds a gold mine, or drills a well for water and discovers oil.

Whatever our urge of growth and self-advancement may be, if we set our mind and heart on some mundane goal, let us pray: *"Father, this is my good as I see it. Nevertheless, I want what in Your sight is best."* This, after all, was Jesus' way of praying, varying only a little the form of His words (which we are so often hesitant to repeat): "My Father, if it be possible, let this cup pass from me: nevertheless, not as I will, but as thou wilt."

So why are we here? I believe we are here by divine direction. As Shakespeare has Hamlet say, "There's a divinity that shapes our ends, rough-hew them how we will."

As a world in which to have everyone approve of us and everything agree with our moods and whims and desires, it is a miserable failure. But as a world in which to learn and grow, it is well-nigh perfect. We attract and are attracted to the people, the places, the lessons, the problems, the opportunities, that offer us the experiences our inmost nature demands. We fulfill our life's purpose—and find that purpose in the process—by accepting life, by proclaiming it good, by agreeing that we are adequate and more than adequate for whatever it demands of us.

You Are Needed

Everyone of us is needed, just as everyone has needs. No life need be so circumscribed by the years, or by real or fancied limitations, as to be without purpose or possibilities of happiness and content. One woman of eighty, living alone and in modest means, conducts an almost worldwide correspondence with people she has never seen. When she reads of someone doing something she approves, she writes to tell him so, often augmenting her personal words by an appropriate quotation in verse or prose. She has letters in response, often so grateful as to suggest that people generally write more letters about things they disapprove than those they like. A younger woman, self-conscious about a minor affliction, tended to avoid people; but she finds fulfillment in reading to the blind—who don't care about her appearance! A man I know has a lot of faith in the younger generation. He celebrates their accomplishments by sending anonymously a dollar bill to outstanding youths he learns about, with a note: "I want you to know that someone has faith in you."

Another friend, close to ninety, has ministered to thousands upon thousands of persons and chafes against relative inactivity. "Oh, Ernest, I'm so old!" she exclaims to me. "That's not your problem, dear," I answer. "You are young, and your body just can't keep up with you!" She laughs in response and goes merrily on.

By Taking Thought

The little woman with the snowy white hair and the snapping black eyes, seated at the editor-in-chief's desk at Unity, read the words over again, repeating them aloud: "Who by taking thought can add one cubit unto his stature?"

"Well, I for one, am going to find out!"

Such a declaration was typical of Imelda Octavia Shanklin, one of Unity's finest editors and writers. And find out she did! She actually increased her height an inch, "by taking thought."

The Revised Standard Version of the Bible, which the present Unity editors prefer, offers a different rendering of the text, making it read: "Which of you by being anxious can add one cubit to his span of life?"

Miss Shanklin was not anxious and she *did* "take thought." She did not add a cubit to her stature. (A cubit, according to Webster, is about eighteen inches). She did not, presumably, add eighteen inches, or eighteen minutes, to her span of life, though how anyone could determine this is past finding out. She did accomplish two very interesting things.

She gave the question concentrated, persistent attention. She actually accepted the challenge of the words as she and most of us have read and interpreted them. She did not just take their significance for granted.

She did add to her physical stature as a result. We can only speculate as to whether in "taking thought" she instinctively sat taller, walked taller, thought taller, which would have been a logical follow-up. And though eighteen inches, added to her five-foot-three-or-so physique, would have been stretching the point to absurdity, she did actually gain an inch in height over a period of weeks.

Would They Come to Dinner?

Another enterprising thinker, a Unity minister who has been enthralled by the life and methods of the great Teacher, became fascinated by Jesus' parable of the king who planned a feast in honor of his son's marriage, and wondered whether his method of meeting a situation would work out today.

For one silly reason or another, those whom the king invited did not respond. They made excuses. Finally, spurred on by their apparent disrespect, the king commanded his servants to go out into the highways and byways and invite whomever they encountered to attend the feast.

The minister understood the symbolical nature of the story: that Jesus, the Savior, invites us to a feast of union with Him, but through stupidity, inertia, disbelief, or lethargy, we do not respond. We sacrifice the real in favor of the apparent, the enduring for the transient, the greater for the lesser.

But what would happen, the minister thought, if the story were to be applied literally in this present day? Suppose he, a minister in a modern American city, were to send his representatives out into the streets and along the waterfront, and offer free tickets to a holiday feast? What would happen? He called a meeting of key men in his congregation and presented the idea to them. They too were fascinated with the possibilities.

To put Jesus' words to the test required activated thought, thought in the form of a definite plan, preparation, imagination, faith, and quite a bit of daring.

Preparing the Way

They envisioned an attendance of several hundred people. A hall with facilities for serving them must be obtained. It was donated. A bakery contributed rolls, and offered to roast the turkeys and hams that would be needed. A dairy contributed milk, cream, butter. Vegetables came from the growers. A printer prepared invitational tickets. Each contribution aroused added enthusiasm among the committee members and contributors. Finally, as the crucial day arrived, the tickets were offered at random to men on the streets.

"What is this, some kind of gyp?"

"Is it for real?" others asked.

"Try it and see!" was the response.

The hour arrived, and with it several hundred men assembled in the hall that had been donated for the occasion. Many arrived early.

Some of them brought guitars. One or two pulled out harmonicas. Soon they were singing, telling stories, and otherwise entertaining themselves while the dinner was being placed on the long tables by volunteering women of the church. Heads bowed reverently when a prayer was offered. Appetites were impressive. Many responded to the invitation for seconds. When all were served to repletion there was still a little food remaining. There had been "enough and to spare."

What was gained by all this? The minister felt that it was a kind of practical Christianity project. Hundreds of his people, and many from beyond his congregation, took part in the enactment of a Scriptural story! Hundreds of men out of work were provided not only with a nourishing meal, but with the intimation that "someone cared"; that for a brief hour at least they answered the age-old challenge, "Am I my brother's keeper?"

"Putting yourself in the story" is an adventure in thought carried over into action that nowadays is often described as "involvement."

"What would happen if——?" often leads to expanded horizons of thinking. In centering your attention on one theme, you discover unexpected variations on the theme, as composers know and illustrate in symphonies and concertos. "Taking thought" is like putting yourself in a stream with many eddies and currents. It is as if you get into a current of thought that you did not so much originate as discover and respond to.

A shrewd little Roman tax collector became curious about the Master Jesus. He put himself "in the way" of finding Him. Being short of stature and thus unable to see over the heads of the crowds that invariably gathered whenever there were rumors of Jesus' appearing, Zacchaeus climbed up into the branches of a sycamore tree overhanging the road by which Jesus would approach. Zacchaeus did not determine the way Jesus would take. He put himself in line with the probability, and consequently saw the Christ. What is more, Jesus saw him, and His response was more than the wily little man could have anticipated.

"Come down out of that tree, Zacchaeus," said Jesus, in effect. "I am coming home to sup with you!"

Something comparable to this happens to innovators

in thought. They start out for one attainment, and often reach other and greater ones.

When You "Take Thought"

To "take thought," as we are considering the expression, means to direct our attention strongly and predominantly to some one line of thinking. But when you do this, you are likely to find that "you get more than you bargained for."

Serendipity

James Watt's curiosity about steam issuing from the spout of a teakettle contributed to the perfecting of the steam engine and its many uses. Newton was curious about the energy involved in an apple's fall and evolved the theory of gravity.

"The key to successful methods," Thomas Edison declared, "comes right out of the air. A real thing like a general idea, a beautiful melody, is pulled out of space—a fact which is inexplicable."

"Ford thought automobiles; Rockefeller thought oil; the Wright brothers, the airplane; Alexander Graham Bell, the telephone; Burbank thought plants, and so a great thought in the mind of a great man can create a new era of living."

Beethoven tells of simply hearing the melodies of his compositions and writing down what he had heard. Mozart was once approached by a young man who wanted to become a composer and thought maybe the master could tell him how. "One doesn't teach how to compose music. One composes because he cannot help it. It just comes."

An extraordinary fact about concentrated thought is that the results do not seem to be exclusive to any one individual. Someone else may have "tuned in" on the same mental concept. One modern musician wrote what he thought was an original melody, only to find that on an occasion when he had the opportunity to examine some rare old manuscripts, someone else had written the same theme almost two hundred years before him. Maeterlinck presents the concept of great souls awaiting a time to be born. Perhaps it is so of great ideas. "There is nothing so powerful as an idea whose time has come." It is as if a great thought, a great idea, is ripe for manifestation, and awaiting any channel that can express it.

The Theory of Evolution

A striking illustration of this possibility is the case of Charles Darwin, usually considered the originator of the theory of evolution, and Alfred Russel Wallace, who conceived the same idea at almost precisely the same time. Darwin wrote to his friend Sir James Hocker, in 1844, "At last gleams of light have come, and I am almost convinced (quite contrary to the opinion I started with) that the species are not (it is like confessing a murder) immutable." By January, 1858, after studying T. R. Malthus' "Essay on the Principle of Population," he began what was to be the definitive statement of his theory. Meantime Alfred Russel Wallace, another distinguished scientist, also began to consider Malthus' "Essay" and during a period of intermittent fever contracted in the South Seas in February of that same year, "there suddenly flashed upon me the idea of the survival of the fittest," he wrote.

The theory was thought out and expanded over the next two days, and sent to Darwin, whom he did not know personally. "Darwin," according to the Encyclopedia Britannica, "at once recognized his own theory in the manuscript essay sent by the unknown naturalist in the tropics, then a stranger to him. 'I never saw a more striking coincidence,' he wrote. 'If Wallace had my manuscript sketch written out in 1842, he could not have made a better short abstract! Even his terms now stand as heads of chapters.' "

The essay was read, along with an abstract of Darwin's own views, as a joint paper before the Linnean Society on July 1, 1958.

Hunches or Impressions

"What is the difference between a thought that comes from your own conscious mind, and a hunch that comes from beyond the conscious mind?" is a question that often perplexes those whose attention is attracted to thought processes.

The difference between your conscious thinking and a hunch is that a hunch is very persistent. Often it is at variance with your own accepted notions of what is a desirable course of action. It may counsel immediate action where this seems rash; it may counsel delay, where immediate action seems imperative. An illustration from actual experience is that of a young minister who was facing a situation which involved members of his family in what amounted to a minor scandal. There was property which he felt must be sold immediately as one major step toward disposing of the matter.

"I cannot go on with my ministry unless this property is sold immediately," he declared. Yet every time he sought to bring about such an outcome it was as if he had a mental block. His mind refused to think clearly.

Other matters insisted on his conscious attention. "This will end my career before it has hardly started," he thought. He couldn't go on. But he did. It was a year before the property was sold. The unhappy incidents were lost sight of by everyone but the young minister, long before the financial and personal involvements were adjusted. And what would have been a serious financial loss if the property had been disposed of earlier became a substantial benefit.

A hunch is very persistent, and will not subside until you either ignore it or act upon it; but usually it speaks in a "still small voice." It is your privilege to reject it, as sometimes in retrospect we realize that we have done, to our regret. "I had a hunch. Why didn't I follow it?" is a frequent lament.

Thoughts that have their origin in your conscious mind or that impinge from external material sources will shift with the winds of expediency; they come and they go. One moment you are confident about them, the next you are unsure. If you want to do a thing and yet feel that you shouldn't, that is a hunch. Try to impersonalize your thought. Imagine someone else coming to you with a similar desire. View it with detachment. Adopt a listening attitude of mind. Say to yourself: *"Father, I want to do whatever is for my good or the good of others, regardless of whether it accords with my personal desires and apparent advantage. Make your guidance very clear and plain, so that though I am as a little child, not knowing how to go out or come in, the darkness shall be as the light, and the next step before me made plain."*

Relax. Be open and receptive. Follow out scrupulously what your hunch tells you to do. Practice doing this whenever a hunch is accorded you. Gradually, by faithful obedience, you will act without hesitation, in the confidence that is born of experience.

Arise and Impinge

Thoughts arise from within us. Thoughts impinge from the world around us. People often "feel poor" even though their personal affairs report abundance, because they react sympathetically to thoughts of recession that are taking form in the mental atmosphere of the world around them. In such an atmosphere the tendency is to curb purchases and expenditures. It is like breathing out and breathing in. When this is done naturally, the circulation is good, and health is promoted. Let a person begin to think consciously and perhaps anxiously about the breathing process, and his breath begins to become restricted. Many forms of illness are readily seen to be the outpicturing of hostilities, fear, resentment, and kindred negations.

Reject such thoughts. Give your rejection a light touch; do not give such thoughts power; realize instead how ridiculous they are. Laugh them out of existence. Remember the couplet, "Death came to the door one day, but heard a laugh and went away." Affirm: *"God is my instant, constant, and abundant supply of all good. As for me and my house, we are the Lord's. All that the Father gives me shall come to me, without haste, without delay, in perfect ways, and under grace."*

As You Sow

Prosperity is an attitude of mind, a state of con-

47

sciousness. In the body-corporate of a nation, prosperity depends largely upon good circulation—a wholesome atmosphere of giving and receiving, breathing out and breathing in. "When things are tight, something has to give. When things are tight, *someone* has to give." The lack that is experienced in a recession is lack of faith. Fear is a restricting, paralyzing emotion. Lot's wife, leaving Sodom but looking back fearfully at the rain of fire upon the city, "froze in her tracks," as a person sometimes does in a terrifying dream. The Bible tells us that she turned into a pillar of salt. In other words, she was petrified with fear. The word *petrified* is significant; it comes from the same root as Peter, *petros* in Greek. Jesus made a play on words when He said of Peter, "On this rock I will build my church."

An old story illustrates what happens in such attitudes of thought as we have described.

The Other Nine Thousand

The Plague came to a certain king one day and said, "I am going into your kingdom today and kill a thousand people." But before the Plague returned to the king, ten thousand had died. The king said to the Plague, "I thought you were only going to kill one thousand of my people." "That's all I killed," the Plague responded. "Fear killed the other nine thousand!"

Change your thought and in effect you change things, for thought forms patterns. "You will decide on a matter, and it will be established for you." (Most people forget the last two words of the statement, and thoughtlessly and unkindly decree bad results to follow the course of action that people among their acquaintance pursue).

"You never can tell what a thought will do,
  In bringing you hate or love;
 For thoughts are things, and their airy wings
  Are swifter than carrier doves.
 They follow the law of the universe—
  Each thing creates its kind,
 And they speed o'er the track to bring you back
  Whatever went out from your mind."

Throw Away Your Crutches

You do not have to be a trained psychologist to see apparent evidence of how thought outpictures in bodily conditions, although being academically trained might prevent you from making a too-easy, too-obvious judgment, when not to pass judgment at all would be better—and passing judgment would only be justified when the purpose was to be helpful, and actually enabled you to be. However some instances of apparent evidence are so obvious that it is difficult to ignore them.

There is, as an example, the case of a woman who felt called upon to welcome her mother-in-law as a member of the household. With something of a martyr spirit, she gave up her own sunny bedroom and moved into the north-exposure guest room. Soon she began to develop a succession of colds. She gave up her room, but seemingly gave herself a congestion.

Then there was the aging professional woman who continually got behind in her financial obligations through poor management of her not inconsiderable income. Her financial reverses were followed by a succession of falls which put her on crutches. She turned

49

for counseling to a metaphysical teacher whose offices were in the same building. "How can I overcome having so many falls?" she demanded of the teacher.

"Throw away your crutches," he responded.

"Oh, I can't do that! I might have another fall!" she exclaimed.

She didn't realize that the teacher meant her mental crutches, of which the physical ones were an outpicturing.

Shutting People Out

There was another woman who, from early years, continually rejected human associations. The contacts would start off promisingly enough, but soon she would begin to see flaws in the speech and behavior of her acquaintances, and would reject their overtures of friendliness. Finally, in what some people call the "sunset years" of life, she had a traumatic experience of being attacked by an intruder and left unconscious. When she was discovered, it was found that her eyesight was affected. Gradually her sight waned until it completely left her. Again, as in earlier years, people tried to be friendly. She rejected their advances, and now, although she is surrounded by other people in the rest home which is her abode, she is in almost complete isolation. A relationship between her physical condition and the mental attitude she had maintained through the years appears obvious. We "cannot shut our eyes" to the inference that she had shut her eyes to overtures from others that were distasteful to her. So the senseless physical attack upon her which triggered her sight impairment seems more like the occasion than the reason for her blindness.

This is an extreme and tragic result of persistently held negative thoughts and emotions, pent up within an individual over a period of years. By the same token, constructive thoughts and feelings may be seen to be strongly conducive to wonderfully good results, as the following account attests.

Love Prospers Any Occupation

A waitress once came to me for help in increasing her income. In the ostentatiously smart eating place where she was employed, the tip potential was much greater than the pay offered by the management. Her tips were not on the scale she felt she had a right to expect.

"Do you enjoy your work?" I asked.

"Enjoy it? No, I hate it—waiting on all those rude, patronizing people. Bad enough under any circumstances, but the tips are so small I can't afford it."

"Then you must either learn to like it, or give up and turn to some other means of livelihood. The way things are now, you are cheating three ways on the job."

"Cheating! What do you mean?"

"First of all, you are cheating yourself."

She nodded agreement to that.

"You are cheating yourself of the pleasure that everyone should find in at least the major portion of his occupation.

"You are cheating the firm that has employed you to serve its customers.

"Worst of all, you are cheating the patrons you serve."

"They get what they deserve," she began, and went on with a recital of the indignities that she felt were heaped upon her. She made me think of the television comedian who "never gets no respect."

"Give them more than you think they deserve, and maybe it will inspire them to better reactions," I suggested.

A counselor's job, as I see it, is more a matter of asking questions, inviting responses, than preaching. In this instance we discussed the three points of view—employer, waitress, customer—with special emphasis on what kind of service one would expect if one were dining in such an establishment.

We talked over things that we thought a customer had a right to expect from a waitress: a pleasant manner, prompt and cheerful service, anticipating the customer's needs before he is aware of them, refilling a water glass, a coffee cup, removing dishes when they are no longer needed. I suggested that she might start the day with a good, strong, affirmative thought, maybe something lighthearted and informal that rhymes and is easy to remember: *"I do a wonderful work in a wonderful way; I give wonderful service for wonderful pay."* I also ventured to suggest that it had taken quite a while for her to get into the state of mind with which the interview started, and that there must be a kind of reconditioning process taking place, as she worked to change her thoughts, and thereby her world.

"Maybe you're not always going to be a waitress. Maybe there are other things for you to undertake; but as long as you *are* a waitress, I suggest you try to be the very best one there is. Remember that it's not only what you do, it's what and how you think and feel about it—how you *act* about it too, oh, very especially that—that is important. Silently repeat that affirmative jingle. Later on you may want to follow it up with the daily lesson from *Daily Word*, maybe tuning in on a dial-a-prayer message as you prepare for work. I see that you do a good job in giving attention to your grooming. Do no less with your attitudes, and you will prosper amazingly.

"Dine out somewhere on your days off. Observe what makes the difference between the best and the poorer eating places—besides the food, that is."

Things turned out even better than she or I could have anticipated. She did learn to find enjoyment in her work. Customers began demanding to be seated at her tables. Her gratuities from grateful diners increased. One appreciative customer found that he just couldn't do without her, and now they are happily married.

But the Truth Is . . .

"A truth to know, and a way to go" is a slogan often heard among Unity students these days; often, too, carried over into action. And no abstract statement of the principle involved ever has quite the impact on our imagination as that of a principle applied in some contemporaneous experience. "How has it worked? How does it work? Will it work for me?" are pragmatic questions that offer adventures in living.

One of the most formidable assertions with which another person can assail us is, "Now I'm going to tell you the truth!" Instinctively we flinch, as from an expected blow, because that assertion almost invariably is the preface to some criticism or accusation. It means that we are going to hear something we would rather not hear, something at least unpleasant, possibly worse than that.

Is the truth, then, so bad to hear? No, the truth is not; but facts may be. Most of what people assert as "the truth" is not even fact, but only opinion. Often the most assertive of our friends, those who state their opinions most strongly, are among the least informed. The vehemence of their assertions is in inverse ratio to the authority that backs up their notions.

In metaphysics one of the things we must learn to do is make a clear distinction between opinions, facts, and truth. "Test everything; hold fast what is good," Paul admonished the Thessalonians. Trying to determine what is a snap judgment, or (hopefully) a carefully considered opinion, or a well-supported fact, calls for the patient but open-minded use of all our mental resources. In situations that reach beyond our immediate world into the larger sphere of community, state, nation, the world, we have to depend upon the various media of communication, and the perspicacity of the writers and commentators; what is implied as well as what is shown in illustrated magazines and on television (and what is left out that might modify what is seen and heard)!

Distinctions between facts and truth represent another plateau of awareness and response: the way we see ourself, or the way someone else may see us.

Perhaps this can be illustrated by what happened to an erstwhile Unity worker when the world headquarters was still in downtown Kansas City. Carrying many responsibilities, he had allowed himself to become despondent over his inability to accomplish all that he felt should be done as promptly as the doing was needed. He left his desk and slipped into the Silent Unity prayer chapel.

Walking on My Heart

It is the custom in Silent Unity for each member to have an hour's prayer vigil in the chapel, so that as one leaves, another soon enters. It was at such a time that our friend entered the chapel. Except for himself it was momentarily empty. He sank into a seat and soon was lost in meditation, when he felt a hand resting gently on his shoulder. It was one of the Silent Unity workers who had come for his hour of prayer.

"Is something troubling you?" he asked.

"I'm walking on my heart!" was the response. Then

followed, in fumbling utterances, the confused recital of what was bothering him.

"You feel inadequate for all that you are called on to do—and do so well? Well, then, let me tell you something. And if I should be the first one to tell you, I will consider it a God-appointed privilege." Then for the next few minutes, this dedicated man told our friend all the good things he had observed about him, all the good things he thought and felt about him, all that he believed the troubled one could yet attain.

"It was a benediction, like a baptism of the Holy Spirit," our friend confesses. "It makes me think of the poem by Richard C. Trench, in which he says in part:

'Lord, what a change within us one short hour
Spent in Thy presence will prevail to make,
What heavy burdens from our bosoms take, . . .
We kneel how weak, we rise how full of power.
Why therefore should we do ourselves this wrong,
Or others—that we are not always strong,
That we are ever overborne with care,
That we should ever weak or heartless be,
Anxious or troubled, when with us is prayer,
And joy and strength and courage are with Thee?' "

The *truth* is the good, the true, the enduring, "the last for which the first was made." The *fact* is what appears to be real to the senses, to the realm of time and space and form; the realm of unremitting change. The truth is that which is eternal, without beginning or end, "birthless, deathless, changeless forever," as Sir Edwin Arnold writes.

The Truth Is—

What are the facts, what is the truth, about the things

that most habitually concern us?

The fact is that you are a physical being, whose body was ushered into this world through the portals of birth, as the result of procreation. You have grown through infancy, childhood, youth. You have been concerned with learning how to use your body and your mind, concerned to get an education, to know the yearnings of the flesh and of the spirit, to fall in love, to marry and start some other souls on the round of experiences, successes, and failures that you have known. You will see them grow, help them, ache for them, try to release them to their own destiny, sense the passing of the years, mark the changes in your own body, know health and sickness, acceptance and rejection, fulfillment and loneliness. You will long to know the meaning of life, and will experience intimations of its meaning. In course of time you will find release from the physical body, and thereby disappear from this mundane world.

What is the truth about all this?

The truth is that you are an individual spark of the Light that lights the life of every man coming into the world, a thought in the mind of God, a drop of water in the sea of infinity, a soul that has taken on a physical body so that it may manifest fact after fact after fact, what is already established as the truth of being, until all facts at last merge into and are seen as the individual experience of the truth. Essentially you are a spiritual being, *created* in the image and likeness of God, but manifesting as a physical being *formed* of the dust of the earth. But "you are dust, and to dust you shall return" was not spoken of the soul.

You are an eternal being whose existence did not begin when you came into this plane of life, and shall not end when you leave it—leave it not to your own extinction, but to your graduation into another plane of existence, there to rest and review what you have done and failed to do, what you have learned and have yet to learn, until you shall feel renewed and refreshed and ready to "take to the road again."

What about your health?

The fact may be that you have a physical challenge; it could be even a frightening one (for it has been said, we are wonderfully and fearfully made). If so, what shall you do about it? Is it practical simply to deny the existence of the problem? Affirm perfect health?

What Each Must Do

You should and must do what is proportionate to your awareness of the action of the creative forces in your being. There are, to repeat, no limitations in Spirit, but there are still limitations to human consciousness; otherwise we might not even be functioning in this plane of being. So while aspiration urges (and should urge) us ever upward in levels of consciousness, common sense suggests that we should not let spiritual pride prevent us from using whatever form of help meets our need. *"Go first direct to God; go next to man and to human agencies as God directs."* There are many channels of healing, but only one Source.

You would not ask if denial and affirmation alone are sufficient to dispel a challenge, unless you both hoped and doubted. If your convictions equaled your aspirations there would be no question. But to do so fearfully may even add to the difficulty by having a

59

mind divided between aspiration and conviction. Maeterlinck presents an episode in his play "The Blue Bird," somewhat related to this concept, where the Fairy says to the boy Tyltyl, "Have I a hooked nose and have I lost one of my eyes?" and Tyltyl tries to be polite in answering: "Oh, no, I can't say that. . . . Who put it out?"

For most of us the practical attitude would be to admit the fact of the obvious, but only as something that has come *to pass*. "Yes, there is a physical problem to be met, but I know that it doesn't have to stay this way. With God's help, and whatever human or mundane channels He may appoint, it can be healed. *God's power is greater than any human or mundane agency, any pill or potion, any manipulation or surgery, although on occasion He may employ any combination of these, as channels suitable to the consciousness of one who seeks the help.*"

What about supply?

It is possible that you need employment, or that your manifest supply is inadequate for your needs. Shall you deny this, tear up the bills, sit idly by and wait "for something to turn up," like Micawber in Dickens' "David Copperfield"? More practical it is to stir up the gift of God that is within us, look within and about us as to our actual and potential resources, "take our sense of need out of isolation," begin with what we have, acclaiming what we have instead of what we apparently lack, and put what we have to use, either more diligently than previously, or in a new way, a new place, toward a different goal. Say: *"Plenty is mine, for I am a child of the Most High. God always has met, and always will enable me to meet, every human need. He opens ways where there seems to my human sense to be no way. I send my loving thought over the barrier of human limitations, and love dissolves barriers, reveals bounty, establishes confidence and enthusiasm. I have faith in God, faith in myself, faith in my fellow men, faith that God can and does work through me to inspire efficient, loving service, generous and bountiful response."*

What about human relationships?

The fact may be that somewhere in ourself or in our associates there is misunderstanding, jealousy, or gossip. How shall we deal with these? The truth is that to try to deal with them by combating them or discussing them only complicates matters. A famous English statesman of a generation or two ago was much troubled by false stories about his personal life. He reacted by having advertisements placed in the leading newspapers, denying the rumors, thereby bringing them to the attention of thousands of persons who had not known about them.

Where There's Smoke

Instead, you might follow the method of a certain minister who was troubled by gossip and an effort to discredit him that seemed to have been inspired by jealousy of his success. "Where there's smoke there must be fire," was one of the comments repeated to him by a well-meaning friend. "Yes," was his response, "but it is well to consider who started the fire."

There remained with him, however, the desire to establish better and more constructive relationships with his peers. How should he deal with the situation?

What would he advise someone else to do if such a problem were placed before him? "I'd tell him to pray about it," was his obvious answer. So that is what he tried to do. But how do you pray for or about people who slander you and seek to destroy you?

"I could not honestly pray that the others would be justified against my own sense of what was true and right. Nor could I, as a minister, pray that I would be vindicated in a way that would humiliate and embarrass them," he explained. At last he released the whole matter and tried to turn his thought entirely to the love, the power, the understanding of God. With this, a way of prayer "came through," as people say. "I can pray that *all things conform to the right thing, under grace and perfect law. The Christ in me greets the Christ in others, and we work together for the glory of God. I do not need to defend myself. If what I am does not speak louder than what I say, then there is a lesson in this for me, and I will find and heed it.*"

He followed this type of affirmation by seeking out good qualities in the persons who opposed him. He did not seek or avoid reference to any of them in conversation. If their names came up, he spoke well of them. He found opportunities to be of service to two or three of the apparent instigators of the rumors. He tried to correct anything in his own behavior that might give credence to their belief. As yet another leader declares, *"I radiate only love and good will, and I accept nothing less from others."*

What about problems?

The fact is that "the only place there are no problems is in the cemetery." As long as we are in this three-dimensional world of experience there will be problems, because this is the schoolroom of life. We have come into this dimension to become in fact what we are in truth; to apply principle to experience. But the seed of the solution is in the problem.

The truth is that a problem is transmuted into an experience, and the experience can be joyous if while we are undergoing it we are at the same time confident, *convinced* that there is a solution to the problem, that we can find it, and that the ultimate outcome will be good. Thus if the ultimate outcome is good, can we logically call the steps that lead to the solution less than good? Take the thought: *By myself, and in my present state of mind, I may not see or know the solution I seek, but God and I together know the answer, and know that the answer is good. So I seek to be so consciously one with God that nothing needful is hidden from me. He brings all things needful to my understanding—the information, the resources, the human personalities to bring about the maximum good results; and this without haste, without delays, in perfect ways and under grace. Though God is never in a hurry, He is always on time.*

About Time

And what about time?

The fact is that in this mundane world, everything takes time. "First the blade, then the ear, then the full grain in the ear." "Bring forth fruit with patience." Consequently nothing outwardly seems to take place as swiftly as it can be conceived in thought. There is a kind of "time lag," which harasses many eager, aspiring souls.

The truth again is that *to Spirit results are instantaneous; to consciousness they are progressive.* To Spirit cause and effect are one; the result preexists in the cause; flower and fruit are one; past, present, and future are one. To earth-consciousness this is difficult to understand, yet there are innumerable illustrations. When you are creatively happy, time flies by. The artist engrossed in putting his vision on canvas, the musician attuned to the music he is putting onto paper, the inventor bringing some new concept into manifestation is oblivious to time, "out of this world," forgetting to eat and drink, even to sleep. Authors, creating characters in a novel or calling forth new concepts of possibly old problems, may tell you that it is not without some difficulty at times that they get into that "other-worldly" creative state of being; that once attained it is a kind of ecstasy, that coming out of it into what we call the actual world is like coming down to a less desirable plane of consciousness.

By the same token, when men are confined, doomed for a time to inactivity, or awaiting the outcome of important issues and decisions that are dependent upon persons and forces outside themselves, time creeps at a snail's pace.

Time appears to expand or contract in relation to our moods.

The Nature of Time

Time is a measure of perception. To some thinkers, both ancient and modern, time is conceived of as the fourth dimension, the next level beyond the realm of three dimensions that characterize the objective world in which for the most part we presently function. Without time, nothing happens in our world. "Time stands still." Manifestation is frozen, the phenomenon we witness on the motion picture or television screen when the camera stops: the moving picture becomes a still picture.

We think of ourselves living in a world of passing time. We say, "Time marches on." The past disappears into nothingness. The future does not exist. What has become of the past? Does it truly not exist? And the future—does it only begin to exist as we enter it, thereby transforming it into the present?

"Let us try to conceive how time can be a dimension," invites Maurice Nicoll. "Let us suppose that we are traveling along this dimension as along a road. We travel from yesterday into today and from today into tomorrow along a distance which appears to us not to exist. We are separated from yesterday by this distance, which is a time distance. Now we realize that distance in space does not mean nonexistence. London is distant from Paris by a space interval of so many miles. Along this distance land, sea, towns, and people are extended, and if we traveled along this distance we would see them. Although we cannot see them now, we believe that they exist. We believe that the known dimensions contain their existence, but we have not this belief of distance in time. We believe that this distance is synonymous with annihilation, nonexistence."

If we were to fly over London and Paris we could see them and all their constituents as coexisting in space. To the concept of time as an extension of space, or a part of higher space, past and future exist simultaneously in time as we observe them to exist in known space. They do not begin to be (except to our physical senses, or as mental concepts) when we come to them. They do not cease to be as we leave them.

Instead of time moving, it is we who are moving through time, spread like a landscape. Past, present, and future are coexistent.

The Book of Ecclesiastes, particularly in the early chapters, appears to suggest this time-space concept. "For everything there is a season and a time for every matter under heaven," and man moves through time, not as through a void but as through a realm of contrasting events or possibilities. "I have seen the business that God has given to the sons of men to be busy with. He has made everything beautiful in its time; also he has put eternity into man's mind, yet so that he cannot find out what God has done from the beginning to the end." Note the expressions "in its time" and "from the beginning to the end." The latter expression recurs elsewhere in Scripture, notably in The Revelation: " 'I am the Alpha and the Omega (A.V., 'the beginning and the end'),' says the Lord God, who is and who was and who is to come, the Almighty."

What Shall We Do about Jesus?

What shall we do about Jesus Christ in this modern, sophisticated age, when mankind attempts to make science a god (which may not be too different from making the state a god, as the communists appear to be doing)?

Shall we take the attitude of denying His existence, asserting that He was a wholly mythological character, a personification of the Sun of God—which was a bright idea of the ancient King Akhenaten of Egypt? And were not the disciples also mythical characters, representing perhaps the twelve signs of the zodiac, through which in a year the sun passes, astrologically speaking?

We could make quite a case for the notion, but it seems somewhat like the rural character who visited a zoo for the first time, and was confronted by the sight of a giraffe. It was easier for the farmer to dismiss this strange creature with the abrasive comment, "There ain't no such animal!" than to rearrange his mental concepts of what animals should be!

Embodiment

Some metaphysicians take refuge—and why should they need refuge?—in the concept that Jesus may or may not have existed as a historical character; that it is unimportant whether He did or not; that what is important is that the Jesus story is intended to convey the message that there is a higher nature in man, which is the Christ nature; that this is the message, thereby relegating Jesus to a sort of Western Union messenger who brings you an important telegram. But Jesus was more than a messenger. Was not He the embodiment of the message?

Or shall we dispose of Jesus by saying, "Well, He probably did exist, and did a lot of good things, which through the superstitions of the times and the credulity of the narrators have been glorified as miracles"?

Or shall we say simply that His message is not relevant to this enlightened age? That modern psychology, sensitivity, the medical arts, and science generally are all the savior we need; that we are learning to master space, and before long will be able to create life artifically, synthetically; that we are learning to prolong life in the body, and may be able to extend it indefinitely by transplants and manmade replacements of outworn organs such as the heart.

There is just enough truth in all these views to make them tenable, at least for a time—until we get into *real* trouble! And how much further must we go in order to recognize real trouble, in this day of material affluence, accompanied by unremitting warfare in one or another or several parts of the world, with overpopulation, air, water, and earth pollution, drug addiction, mental illness, violence in the streets, on the campuses, even within the family circle?

No Wonder

But it is no wonder all men cannot seem to accept Jesus Christ!

What manner of man is it who could say that the fields are ripe to the harvest, when your own senses would tell you the harvest is yet four months away;

Who could tell the disciples to break five loaves and

two fishes, small enough for a youngster to tuck in his sleeves, and share them to feed five thousand;

Who could say of a man born blind, "It was not that this man sinned, or his parents, but that the works of God might be made manifest in him";

Who in the face of His enemies could say, "Do you think that I cannot appeal to my Father, and he will at once send me more than twelve legions of angels?"

Who had "nowhere to lay his head," had no possessions, no houses and lands, no stocks and bonds, yet wore a robe so valuable that soldiers cast lots to possess it;

Who could change water into wine to save a hostess embarrassment at a wedding feast;

Who could heal the sick, raise the dead, cast out devilish spirits from a demoniac;

Go through the torture of crucifixion and entombment, yet raise His body again to life, and take it with Him into another dimension of being!

From another place and another time the words of the Psalmist echo with relevance—and reverence too: "Such knowledge is too wonderful for me; it is high, I cannot attain it."

No wonder that some people should say that He was very God, and that others should say that He was the only begotten Son. With this it is easier to agree than disagree, to affirm than to deny, for in Him we see the complete man, in full command, able to do all manner of wonderful things that the rest of us do incompletely or imperfectly. Yet He Himself said that the things He did we should do also, and even greater things. "God," says Charles Fillmore, "has but one Son, the Christ, the one ideal man; the unfoldment of this consciousness of Jesus made Him God incarnate, because Christ is the mind of God individualized."

All Things to All

He is all things to all men who have allowed themselves to relate to Him. He is the doctor, the psychologist, the metaphysician, the preacher, the teacher, the storyteller, the lawyer, the agitator, the redeemer. He is in you and you are in Him, and it is sometimes difficult to know where one leaves off and the other begins. It makes me think of a greatly dedicated man who once worked in Silent Unity, the prayer ministry of the Unity Movement. It was his privilege and duty to answer phone calls during the night from people who asked for prayers. Sometimes he would be so deep in meditation that when he made a notation of the request, to which he was supposed to sign his name, he would write "Jesus" instead of his own name, Joseph!

The only way to dispose of Jesus is to ignore Him as long as possible.

Don't read His story.

Don't think about Him.

It is dangerous to your disbelief.

Beware lest He win you to belief, and then you'll have the responsibility of that belief, and feel that you should do something about it, feel guilty if you don't; and ultimately have to reeducate yourself, readjust your sense of values, and your sense of direction.

Put Yourself in the Picture

Common sense teaches us that to find out the truth about anything is to put ourself in "the way of finding it"—not to close our mind against it.

70

If you really want to find out whether Jesus was real or an imagined person, whether He was like or different from other men, put yourself "in the way" of finding out. There is no way, you say? Perhaps there is. Here is an approach you might try. But do it at the risk of having to modify your present views. Be fair.

It is, quite simply, this: *Put yourself in the picture.*

Turn to the Gospels, preferably in a red-letter New Testament, which presents only the words of Jesus in red. Picture the incident described. Who are present? What are their actions and/or reactions? Who is speaking? What is the setting?

House, temple, marketplace? Stone, brick, wood? Are there paved streets, or dirt roads? The desert, the mountains, a city of the seashore, or on the sea? Is it winter, summer, spring, fall? Are there trees, shrubs, grass, flowers?

If there is movement, as in traveling from one place to another, picture yourself in the scene. Is Jesus there? Can you picture Him? What is the expression on His face? Serene, joyous, meditative, pensive, sorrowful? As He speaks, what is the tone of His voice? The look in His eyes? Does He ever smile?

As Glover wrote, in his "The Jesus of History":

"Here is a suggestion which we find true in ordinary life as well as in the study of literature (the Gospels). If we turn it back upon its author, he at least will not complain, and we shall perhaps gain a new sense of his significance by approaching him at a new angle, from an outlook not perhaps much frequented. How does he come to speak in this manner, say this and that? To what feeling or thought, to what attitude to life, is this

71

or the other saying due? If he, too, spoke 'out of the overflow of his heart'—and we can believe it when we think of the freshness and spontaneity with which he spoke—of what nature and of what depth was that heart?"

Stranger than Fiction

A good novelist can make a fictitious character seem so real that someone who doubts the historicity of Jesus may well question whether His story is not such a skillful fabrication. But surely if so, the writer could have done a better job. They could at least have been consistent, as a clever writer tries to be. That they are not is, we might conclude, evidence that they are true. For people do not all see the same thing the same way.

Have you ever heard evidence in a court trial, or read it in the press? How differently witnesses see, or think they have seen, the circumstances! It is not that they are dishonest, it is that they see with their minds and emotions—and with memory that borrows a little from other experiences than the one at issue. Matthew, Mark, and Luke, though they vary in the details of narration, report a common view, and for that reason their accounts are called the Synoptic Gospels. But John's viewpoint was notably different. Whereas they saw Jesus very humanly, John saw Him as a mystical, extra-dimensional figure: man but more than man.

As men of today, we see in Jesus what we are prepared to see. The agnostic Ingersol said, "A man thinks not as he would, but as he must," and Ruskin, expatiating on works of art, says a man more often judges himself by his comments on a work of art, than the work of art upon which he comments. And "the greatest thing a human soul ever does in this world is to *see* something, and tell what it saw in a plain way. . . . To see clearly is poetry, prophecy, and religion, all in one."

How do you "see" Jesus?

Divinely Human

When most men think of Jesus the Christ, they seem to picture a man, bearded, serious, haloed: "a man of sorrows, and acquainted with grief." They think of Him in His divine aspect, as a great teacher performing miracles, living a life that, because of His divinity, must have been quite different from that of other men. They forget that Jesus was human as well as divine. They forget that He spent a number of years in the process of growing up, very much like any other boy.

If we remember this, we will see in the discourses of His manhood many indications of the nature of that boyhood. We will derive a new sense of His oneness with us, not only by reason of a mystic spiritual unity but because His experiences were so natural, so human, so real, so very much like what our own might have been in His day, or even very much like what our own are in this day.

Jesus was a small-town boy, son of the village carpenter. Much more than this He was, as the patient years have revealed. But in the years of His boyhood, there were few who guessed Him to be a great teacher, savior of the world. He was simply the eldest child in the large family of Joseph and Mary. No doubt, like other boys, He fetched and carried wood and water. Surely the good clean smell of lumber, the smooth bite of plane and ax, must have fascinated Him. With the lively enthusiasm of youth, He must have mastered the secret

73

of His father's tools and, like other small boys, looked with boyish admiration upon His father's skill, resolving in His heart that when He grew up He would be like him.

The Boy of Nazareth

This boy of Nazareth was interested in out-of-door things, too: in the sparrows that were sold in the marketplace, the lilies in the field, the foxes and their nests, the sheep and their shepherds. One of the loveliest pictures in the discourses of His manhood is drawn from a picture that may well have been recorded upon His mind in youth. He was interested, as travelers in the Orient today are interested, by a certain scene in shepherd life. Often the flocks of several shepherds will be led into a common sheepfold for the night. In the morning they must be sorted out, to roam the hills again in the eternal march for food. But the shepherds do not scramble wildly among the animals to sort out and segregate their charges. It is all much simpler and much more fascinating than that.

Each shepherd has his own distinctive call. The sheep of his flock learn to know this call. When the time comes for them to follow their leader back to the hills, each shepherd in turn stands at the door of the fold and calls. All the sheep prick up their ears, but only those that belong to his flock will move toward him. The rest remain as they are.

When the little boy of Nazareth had become the strong Man of Galilee and wished to illustrate the fact that not everybody was ready to accept His message, but that those who were ready would recognize and respond to it, He remembered the scene in the sheepfold, a scene familiar to virtually every one of His hearers.

"My own know me," He said. "They will heed my voice."

We can picture this same great Teacher as a lad, when He sat, elbows on knees, chin cupped in His hands, on a little stool in the kitchen of His father's house. His father was, perchance, working in his shop adjoining the room, so that the pungent smell of the fresh-cut wood mingled with that of the smoke from the kitchen oven, while Jesus' mother mixed yeast in dough, and put the dough to rise in great pans near the oven. Soon, He knew, the dough would be risen, and His mother would shape it into big loaves, with maybe a little one for Him. The loaves would be put into the oven to bake, and would be brought out, brown and crunchy and savory, to stir a boyish appetite that needed no stirring.

When, years later, He wanted to make plain to His followers what the kingdom of heaven was like, He remembered that scene and dramatized it in the parable of the meal in which a widow hid some yeast that leavened the whole lump of dough. The kingdom of heaven, He made them see, was like that: it increased. It was, in a way of speaking, contagious: a little of it would spread and leaven a whole group of people, a whole community, perhaps the whole Jewish race.

The practical nature of Jesus' teachings, His ability to reach through nonessentials to the core of a matter, wonderful to us in this day, must have been more wonderful, even startling, to the men of the day in which He came. Whereas the wise old theologians of the day debated abstract questions such as, perhaps, how many angels could sit at one time on the head—or was it the point?—of a pin, Jesus brought them back to earth by such practical teachings as these: If you know the Truth you are blessed by using it ("If you know these things, blessed are you if you do them"); and worship to God means brotherhood to man ("So if you are offering the gift at the altar, and there remember that your brother has something against you, leave there your gift before the altar and go; first be reconciled to your brother, and then come and offer your gift"). His straightforward, informal method of teaching must have seemed revolutionary to men accustomed to the circumlocutions of the orthodox priests.

Even the disciples of John the Baptist were troubled, although it is reasonable to imagine that John was very friendly to Jesus' teachings. "Why do we and the Pharisees fast, but your disciples do not fast?" they asked Jesus.

In Jesus' answer, fashioned out of the experience of His life, we see again the lengthened shadow of a little boy at home and in the marketplace of Nazareth. Perhaps as He answered He too saw the little boy He had been.

Patches

The first picture His answer calls up is that of a lad who must have watched his mother mending his clothes and those of his brothers and sisters. In the home of a village carpenter there must have been many patches.

The boy Jesus learned, perhaps from his own boyhood experience, that for his mother painstakingly to put patches of new cloth upon worn-out garments was a waste of time.

To try to put new patches upon the wornout garments of religious custom was equally useless.

We therefore hear Him answering, "No man puts a piece of unshrunk (new) cloth on an old garment, for the patch tears away from the garment, and a worse tear is made."

Again we see the same little boy in the marketplace, round-eyed with wonder at the ways and dress and possessions of travelers passing through the village, or curious about and interested in the village talk and happenings. We can imagine Him before a wineseller's where a crowd has gathered to chuckle as they observe the merchant's discomfiture over a broken wineskin, and to mourn over the wine spilled.

"Why did the wineskin burst?" the boy asks.

"Why, the silly man put new wine into an old skin. Naturally, the old skin was not so strong as when it was new, and the new wine burst it. Too bad to waste good wine that way."

Now, as He talks to the followers of John, we hear Him saying, "Neither is new wine put into old wineskins; if it is, the skins burst, and the wine is spilled, and the skins are destroyed; but new wine is put into fresh wineskins, and so both are preserved."

So, He implied, new ideas such as His own demand new customs.

There are those who say that Jesus is a myth, that He never really lived, that the Gospels are compiled from legend. The Gospels themselves are living testimony to His life. No man fabricating a messiah would use such illustrations as Jesus used. They are taken from a life that was lived. They breathe of living, actual experience. They have the common touch. The religions of the East abound in elaborate symbolism, in flowery metaphor, in involved, abstract ideas. Jesus spoke directly, "as one who had authority, and not as their scribes."

He did have authority, not only the authority of divinity but that of experience as well. No one reading the Gospels with this thought in mind can question their actuality.

Jesus lived! Of that there can be no question. The pictures the Gospels paint could not have been drawn from lifeless symbols. They are the pictures of a vital and forceful personality. Even the formal, dignified style of the writers could not conceal that personality. It shines out at us, sparkling, incisive, definite, in such pictures as these: the call of the shepherd, the yeast in the dough, the patches in old clothes, new wine in old wineskins.

Jesus lived! Evidently He lived in Palestine, despite many theories that He went to India and Egypt during the years between His twelfth and His thirtieth birthday. If indeed He did travel afar, He kept His speech and the illustrations that He used singularly free from the influence of His travels, and singularly rich in the experience of His own country, His own people, His own boyhood village.

Whatever else contributed to His background of wisdom and compassion, it was to the simple things of everyday life—things as simple and human and humdrum as those we experience day by day—that He turned for material with which to illustrate His teachings. His great spirit imbued them with a charm so compelling that we almost lose sight of their simplicity. Not an incident or a figure appears in His teachings that could not be appreciated by all His hearers. Not the experience, but only the vision to interpret, was what had eluded them.

The Many Sides of Man

If you should welcome questions from earnest students, it might surprise, delight, and even astound you at times to find what people want to know about.

It may have been the chapter "Twelve and One," from my book *The Emerging Self*, that inspired the following question from a Unity ministerial student:

"With which one of the twelve disciples do you identify most?"

The personality and character of Jesus fascinate me. His message? Yes, of course, but also the manner of Man behind the message. Would there, could there, have been the message without the Man? In the same vein of thought, I wonder about the twelve men who trudged the hills and valleys of Palestine with Him, ate with Him, lived with Him, slept with Him, questioned Him, loved Him, learned of Him, came out of weakness into strength, from ragged, wavering belief into steadfast faith, from personal differences into unified accord.

What were they like, these rugged men, fishermen mostly? What did Jesus see in them, they in Him? What do you see in them? What do I? Much as I have thought about, mused over them, I had never taken the approach, "With which one do you identify most?"

There is something of the nature of each of the Twelve in each of us. Our eternal self is like a jewel of many facets, and the light of a single lifetime may bring out the brilliance of a single facet, or even several different facets in succession. Yet the overall nature of an individual life may seem to be related to a sign of the zodiac, or to one of the twelve qualities or powers of mind with which spiritual teachers and mystics associate the Twelve. The Bible student may well relate to one or another Bible character at different times in his life, or even in different moods, for *one of the things that makes the Bible a book for all times is that it is so much a book of human nature.* It is the spiritual history of mankind: Man, his-story. Some time or other we play all the parts. With spiritual insight we may well say, "There but for the grace of God go I," or "There *in* the grace of God go I." The overall character of a lifetime predominantly expresses one theme. So it was with the Twelve.

People will argue over whether the Twelve were flesh-and-blood persons like you and me, or whether they were symbolical characters.

Revelation and Excavation

Maybe one of these days scholarship and/or inspiration will settle the matter, as both have contributed to an understanding of the so-called Essenes. By many scholars they were thought to have been merely a legendary cult. Prophecy declared that an Essene community would be found between Jericho and the Dead Sea. Excavation confirmed the prediction. That buried community, called the Qumran Community, has been unearthed at a point only a stone's throw from the cave in which the first of the Dead Sea scrolls were found, enclosed in pottery jars by the very people whose existence had been questioned.

Meanwhile, "With which of the twelve disciples do

you identify most?" Let us consider it together.

The Silent Ones

Are you like one of "the silent ones," such as James, son of Alphaeus, or Simon Zelotes? They are not unimportant characters. None of the Twelve was unimportant. Just being one of the few drawn from the many made each one of them important. In the accounts given in the Gospels there are only meager hints as to their nature. Many wonderful and remarkable people of today may make only a meagerly recognizable impress upon history. It is not that they are unimportant; only that their importance escapes notice and acclaim.

What do we know about this James, called "James the Less" to distinguish him from James the brother of John, and James the brother of Jesus? "Less" possibly also because by implication he may have been small of stature. Are you like him, one of the quiet ones to whom nobody pays much attention?

Or are you like single-pointed Simon who was called the Zealot, "a man who had only one strong motivation"? He was a patriot. He had strong feelings. He was a kind of revolutionary, you might say. Was this what drew him to Jesus? Jesus in His own way was a kind of spiritual revolutionary, and His inspiration transformed the revolutionist into an evangelist. A single-pointed man like Simon can be a power for good when his single-pointedness is aimed in the right direction.

A Man with Three Names

Then there was Thaddaeus, known also as Lebbaeus, and as Jude, or Judas ("not Iscariot," as John says). He was not much of a speaker. He is only quoted once in the Gospels, when he asked Jesus, "How is it that you will manifest yourself to us, and not to the world?" And to this Jesus replied, "If a man loves me, he will keep my word, and my Father will love him, and we will come to him and make our home with him." Thaddaeus, like many of us today, was evidently better at writing than talking, for he is often identified by scholars as the writer of the short but fiery book of Jude, which comes just before The Revelation.

If you feel things intently, and tend to feel that your opinions are indisputable, you might feel a sympathetic kinship to Thaddaeus.

Judas Iscariot

Probably none of us would willingly identify with the unhappy role of Judas. Yet have you never been tempted to make the end justify the means, committing yourself to some course of action that in itself you know is unworthy, for the sake of a good purpose? Never skirted the law, cut corners, practiced a minor or even major deceit? Never been moved to justify yourself by the sorry cry, "I only meant to help a cause by what I did"? Never thereby betrayed those whom you loved and who loved you? One modern-day student has been so greatly moved by the tragic figure of Judas that in an endeavor to understand why he did what he did, he came to believe that he was actually the reincarnation of the Betrayer. Much spiritual counseling was required to free him from the obsession.

Such dark thoughts, in which we might picture ourself enacting a role of evil, does not mean that we are going to act out such a fantasy. Quite the opposite tends to be true. People, I believe, do not usually plot doing an evil thing. They mean to do good, and fall into the trap of wrong methods to attain it. So such dark thoughts should serve the same purpose as red lights or other signals at a street intersection: they can protect us against careless or unwitting missteps. They can help us to determine what, out of all the possibilities of human expression, shall reign in consciousness. Judas was not all evil. He is thought to have been the best educated and most sophisticated of the Twelve; and therein both his strength and weakness resided. How different might his story have been if strength had won!

Thomas, the Deliberate

Are you one who longs to believe in spiritual things, yet finds himself always analyzing, always questioning? If so maybe you would feel sympathetic toward and identify with Thomas. He is typical of all of us who become known to our family, our friends, or even the world for one mistake, rather than for any number of unimpressive but worthy accomplishments. So Thomas, who wanted so much to believe (and did in the ultimate) gained the sobriquet of "doubting Thomas" . . . and thereby becomes one with the football player who ran the wrong way, the singer who flatted the one high C, the politician who named a rival city as the one he was glad to be in!

Bartholomew

Nathanael was somewhat like that, too. His surname was Tolemai, hence as we have explained elsewhere, he was called Nathanael Bar-Tolemai: thus, Bartholomew. He was from Cana in Galilee, the town in which Jesus performed His first miracle. Cana is only eight miles from Nazareth. There was a rivalry between the two towns such as in modern times there has been between San Francisco and Los Angeles, St. Louis and Kansas City—which may have had something to do with his question, "Can any good come out of Nazareth?" Truly, Nazareth did not have a very good reputation. So if you identify with Nathanael, remember that Lincoln was born in a log cabin and made such abodes illustrious: many a singer and artist came from "the wrong side of the tracks."

Try like Nathanael to transform prejudice to piety, so that the Christ in you may proclaim you to be like him, "without guile."

Philip

It was Philip who brought Nathanael to Jesus, after he himself had been convinced that Jesus was indeed the promised Savior or Messiah. Philip has been called the Plodder. One commentator has said that Peter always leaped before he looked, and Philip looked before he leaped. He was the pragmatist among the Twelve. When Nathanael expresses a thoughtful doubt, Philip responds with the pragmatic answer, "Come and see!" In the present time someone might call Philip "the man from Missouri, the Show-Me State." He was deliberate in his decisions, but once convinced, he had the courage of his convictions.

Matthew

Maybe you are more like Matthew. He was a businessman, a collector of customs. He sat at a kind of crossroads of the world of that era, in a toll office on the Mediterranean-Damascus road, where he had every opportunity to observe men of all types and races. He might remind present-day travelers of customs inspectors, those keen-eyed men who seem able to size a man up at a glance. So when Jesus invited him to leave his work and follow Him, he did so without hesitation, in a moment. He was elated to be chosen, and (characteristically) celebrated the occasion of his "spiritual birthday" by giving a party. Long after his meeting with Jesus he gave the world something better than a party—the Gospel that bears his name.

James and John, Brothers

Matthew was probably the wealthiest of the Twelve, with the possible exception of James and John, the sons of Zebedee, a well-to-do fishing merchant.

Probably most of us would like to identify with James or John. They were impetuous men in their youth, hurling down imprecations upon those with whom they differed, not only hoping but expecting special consideration from Jesus, considering it their appointed role in life to rule. And favored they were. They were present at most of the important events in Jesus' ministry: the feeding of the five thousand, the raising of Tabitha, Jairus' daughter, from death to life, the stilling of the storm on the Sea of Tiberias, the time of prayer in the garden of Gethsemane, the Mount of Transfiguration, the healing of the demoniac. As one of the three of the inner circle about the Master, we see James largely in relation to John, as we see Andrew in the shadow of Peter.

Like John, he had a temper, quick to arise, and as quick to subside. But the rashness of James became tempered with the years, as his passion for prominence subsided, so that we think of him as a kind of elder statesman in his maturity, expressing tolerance and judgment.

His brother John, youngest and fairest of the Twelve, modified emotion into devotion. He was the one "whom Jesus loved," and is so referred to six times in the Gospel that he later wrote.

With Peter, the two brothers were members of the trio that led in most of the disciples' activities. Carl Sandburg once said, "We all want to play Hamlet." Peter typifies those who want to be "the best of anybody," who want to play all the parts in the drama, who many times fail but press on past failures, who attain with effort, but are given "the keys to the kingdom." In the beginning Peter had been known as Simon Barjona—or as we would say, Simon, John's son. Jesus gave him the name *Peter*, which means "rock," and in a playful mood, made a pun upon his name (which can mean not only "rock" but "a dull fellow"): "On this rock will I build my church."

Andrew, Introducer

There remains for us to consider, then, one other member of the Twelve: Andres, Peter's brother. Andrew seems always to stand in the shadow of his brother's more ebullient personality. Standing so, yet not standing still, for he more than any of the others was the one who brought men to Jesus. His features are dim to our sight. His deeds stand forth clearly. "I cannot think clearly how he looks, I can only see his good works," is the comment of a modern student about a contemporary teacher. "In his presence I lose sight of him, and see the Master." Many of us could wish to identify with Andrew, in something of the spirit of the saying, "I'd like to be a rose, but if I have to be a dandelion instead, I want to be the best blamed dandelion there is!"

Finally, we may welcome the admonition, "Consider all things; hold fast that which is good," and say a prayer like this:

Help me, O Lord, to be an overcomer; to acknowledge my need without being overcome by it, neither exaggerating or minimizing faults or virtues; learning what to avoid in others' apparent frailties, taking courage from qualities recognized and attained; joyously acknowledging my oneness with all men and my uniqueness under God, with whom all things good become possible and only the good is enduringly true.

You Asked for It

If someone were to ask you, "What, out of all the things you believe, think, know, do you most rely on?" what would be your answer?

I would have to say: "The law that Jesus taught, that science and human experience confirms—the law of cause and effect, of equivalence, action and reaction; taught by Jesus and stated succinctly by Paul in his letter to the Galatians when he says, 'Whatever a man sows, that he will also reap.' "

Is not this a harsh and incomplete statement of spiritual truth? It may seem so, because we immediately think of it in terms of our shortcomings, our mistakes and failures, and the warning that every jot and tittle of the law must be fulfilled. (Even that expression, *jot and tittle,* may trouble us. So look up the words: "jot: (Gr. iota, the smallest letter of the alphabet). An iota; a point; a tittle." "Tittle: A point or small sign used as a diacritical mark in writing and printing. A particle; a minute part; a jot.")

But if this be true of what is contrary to the plan of life ("God saw everything that he had made, and behold, it was very good"), how truly true it must be of everything that is "very good." In other words if evil surely begets evil, must not good surely beget good?

Back of every effect in life lies a finer cause, and each such cause is the effect of a finer cause that preceded it; so that ultimately all things are seen to be the effects of one Cause in which they exist. Effect and cause are as

91

inseparable as sunlight and the sun which is its source. Separate a ray of sunlight from its golden source in the heavens and it ceases to be sunlight; it has no existence apart from that which gave it being. So it is with all else. Effects are distinct from their cause, yet exist only by reason of the cause which preceded them.

Two Worlds

The material world is a world of effects, of forms, or what is commonly called "matter." It is a world of infinite variety, in which many elements seem to be manifested. They appear in the mineral, vegetable, and animal kingdoms, and in the manifold expressions of number, color, sound, and form within these realms. They appear wherever the physical senses of man meet a response; and yet when they are closely examined, all these elements are seen to merge into one—one common stuff, as Emerson put it—one element which is common to all, the essence of all, and without which nothing that exists can have being; an essence that permeates and animates all things yet is distinct from that which it permeates and animates.

Men have called this intangible all-pervading essence Spirit, God, Divine Mind, the Creative Principle.

It is the first Cause in relation to which all manifestations of life, substance, and intelligence are effects.

There exists between God and the manifest creation the same relation that exists between cause and effect, action and reaction. They are the two halves of one thing. Matter is the garment of God; the means by which Spirit expresses; the emanation of the great Positive Mind. Manifestation is the outer form of which spirit is the inner reality. The purpose of form is to express sequentially—that is, through time and space which are characteristics of manifestation, the powers and perfection of deity.

Undeveloped Good?

The system of the universe presents the action and reaction of immutable law by which the infinite perfection of the Cause is evolved through finite manifestation. These expressions of life, motion, sensation, and intelligence lead progressively from one to another like notes in a musical scale. From the lowest, least expressive form of life to the highest, all are obedient to the same laws of being. Each manifests some attribute of the Divine. Nothing is wholly evil, for all are animated by the same essence. What we call evil is undeveloped good. From the protoplasmic cell and the isolated electron, through all the gradations of the three kingdoms to man, each form is in some degree the possessor of the one central essence; each expresses some idea which by reason of its source is divine.

"All are but parts of one stupendous whole,

Whose body nature is, and God the soul."

The principle is simple; the ramifications are multifarious. We look for the causes back of things "that do appear" and we observe caution lest in our zeal we are too hasty and superficial in judgment; too quick to pass judgment on others or ourself. It has been said that "to know all is to forgive all." Certainly *in evaluating an instance of what we call failure we must take into account many good efforts that possibly never quite reached fruition, yet have made their contributions to soul growth.*

So if we do not, seemingly cannot, see the reason,

93

the cause, for some of our present-life experiences, we may be very sure that there is a cause. So universally do we observe the action of this law that in the apparent exceptions that occur in our own life or that of other persons, we know it must be equally true. The cause may be hidden, or may be so remote in the time-space sense that we cannot relate to it, but it exists. The effect attests to cause, as surely as the appearance of a hand attests to the arm, the body, the person of which it is a part.

We may have to disabuse our mind of many old ideas and preconceptions in order to accept completely the basic principle of cause and effect. *Karma* is its ancient name. If we seek the Truth we must follow wherever it leads. We cannot expect it to conform to any manmade creed or doctrine simply because we are accustomed to such traditions.

Remember Me?

Perhaps we can see it better by example than by precept. For instance:

Recently a man whom I had not seen for several years appeared at my study door—it is usually open—and greeted me: "Remember me?"

The voice was familiar but I had to look at him for some moments before I recognized him. He had changed so much.

For the better.

Some people seem to change for the worse with the passage of many years. Some change so little that we marvel. But this man had changed for the better. He not only looked younger, he looked happier. He stood erect whereas I remember him as stooped, despondent, grim-visaged.

"You look great. What has happened to you?"

"It is something you said in a sermon. I challenged it at the time. I thought you were putting it on a little thick. But gradually I came to realize that what you said was true, and that I could—and had better—do something about it!"

"What in the world did I say?" I asked.

"You said, and I believe you said you were quoting somebody else, that *every man makes his own heaven and his own hell and walks an angel or a devil therein.*"

He pulled a sheet of paper from his coat pocket.

"Here, I've jotted down some of the simple thoughts that came to me as I began working on the idea you had planted in my mind:

"*No matter who you are, if you push the right button the light will come on.*

"*Take a crack at somebody and you'll get it right back, either from him or somebody else.*

"*Say, 'If I were he, I would certainly do things better,' and it's like sending out an application for that kind of an experience.*

"*Play with fire and you will get burned.*

"*Ignore the traffic rules and you're inviting trouble; keep on and you're sure to get it.*

"*Knock a competitor's product and the prospect may wonder why you feel you have to.*

"*No matter what anybody tells you, you cannot get something for nothing.*

"*I wondered why nobody ever gave me credit for a job well done, until I realized that I took other people for granted.*

"No matter where I went, what I did, reactions were the same, until I realized it was I who determined what kind of people and situations I met.

"When I wanted more heaven and less hell, I found the only way to get it was to try to make it so for people around me."

Give 'Em Heaven

He grinned and I looked up from reading. "I used to give 'em hell. Now I try to give 'em heaven!" he commented.

"On you that looks good," I responded. "I'd like to use you as Exhibit Number One in my Master Class series."

Simple? Rudimentary? You could find something like this in any one of a score of paperbacks? Maybe so, but as a publisher once told me, these publications are "dream books." People buy them and take satisfaction from reading them and imagining themselves as successful examples of what the books assert. In most cases that is as far as it goes—only as far as wishful thinking. But here standing before me was a living, breathing, flesh-and-blood he-man who had done what others only dreamed about.

"It's worked well for you," I said.

"Very well indeed. It's made me $7,000,000!"

This mundane world is a world of learning in the school of experience. The only trouble, as someone has said, is that you're almost too old to benefit from it by the time you've graduated. Actually, we are never too old, and I don't know of anybody who has graduated, although some seem to have "quituated."

As I have often said in sermons and classwork, *this*

world is far from perfect as a realm in which to have everyone and everything agree with us, but is is a well-nigh perfect world in which to learn and grow.

We have come here from another realm to try out by experience what is conceived to be true in spirit. We should like to think that we are very good students, that all we need is to have something pointed out to us once, and we will have learned what the experience offers and never have to repeat it.

But is this so?

No, it is not. Most of us have repeated cycles of experience.

What You Send Out

In my first year's ministry, I met a woman whom I had known during the time when I was preparing for the ministry. In that earlier acquaintance she was a young divorcee. She had become infatuated with and married a young man who had a great deal of charm but a great deal less practicality. After getting a job herself, and counting on him to do his part, she found he was quite content to let her do it all herself. So she left him.

"The next time I marry, I'm going to look before I leap. I'm going to find somebody of means, maybe older than myself, who will support me in the style to which I would like to become accustomed." Somewhat cynically she added, "I've been told it is just as easy to love a rich man as a poor man, and a lot more comfortable."

That is what she attempted to do.

I say attempted. At first it looked as if in her new setting she had succeeded. She emanated an atmosphere of self-satisfaction. Her husband was indeed wealthy, the owner of a prosperous retail furniture establishment. He was considerably older than she, and the prospects of his demise within a few years and herself as a still fairly young—and prosperous—widow seemed promising. She tried, I think, to be a good wife to him. But the curious outcome was that she was suddenly taken ill and expired. He remained a vigorous and amative man, and soon found solace for his bereavement in another marriage. Without passing judgment, we might be inclined to say that what she sent out returned to her in kind.

We see instances of such actions and reactions in the lives of people all about us. Can it be that we ourself are an exception?

The law of equivalence, compensation, action and reaction is everywhere evident. We sometimes say of somebody that he is lucky, but something within us belies the assertion. "Chance is direction that we could not see." For instance, the father of a very successful theatrical producer (in a realm where to the uninitiated "luck" might appear to be very much a factor) acknowledged the congratulations of a friend on the son's success.

"Your son is certainly very lucky!" was the comment.

"Yes, and I've noticed that the harder he works, the luckier he is."

An apt response, but one on which we do not rely completely, for many of us know of people who work very hard but are not outstandingly successful, at least in their own or the world's opinions. There is more to it than that. Maybe what we call "luck" is simply a way of trying to account for a seemingly unjustified outcome, good or bad.

Any occurrence or condition that appears in manifestation proclaims thereby an antecedent cause, whether known or unknown. As we have said, a hand testifies to an arm of which it is an extension, or a fruit proclaims the tree from which it came. Things do not just happen. They result.

By extension we see that what happens in the particular, as to a certain person or in a specific situation, is true of families, communities, states, and nations. Although generally events in our life are related to causes that we ourself have initiated, wittingly or unwittingly in this life or in a more remote life, and to a greater or lesser degree, we are all involved in the *karma* of our family, our community, our nation.

It may well be considered good fortune to be born into the United States, probably the most affluent of nations, with degrees of liberty that we believe are seldom to be found elsewhere on the earth. But we also have a responsibility thereby. We are creating both good and bad karma by our use or abuse of these privileges; a responsibility that is inescapable under the law of the creative forces of Being. As the Master has said, "Every one to whom much is given, of him will much be required."

Supposers

Annie Besant once remarked that sometimes a theory is very helpful in bridging a gap of unfinished thought. The inquisitive mind of man is uncomfortable in harboring questions for which it has found no answer. This fact undoubtedly plays a big part in "setting the stage" for invention and discovery.

"Suppose," says the mind of Albert Einstein, "that space is not straight but curved," and he comes up with the theory of relativity.

"Suppose," thinks Charles Darwin, "that man was not created and formed entirely independently of the other denizens of earth; that those days of creation were not twenty-four-hour days, but vastly longer," and he comes up with the theory of evolution.

"Suppose I could catch lightning from the sky and put it in a jar," Benjamin Franklin surmises, and he thereby ushers in the age of electricity.

Thomas Edison wonders if he can capture a human voice in wax and persuade it thereby to repeat itself, and the phonograph is born.

The Wright brothers not only dream every boy's dream of being able to rise above the things of earth, but contrive wings and a motor to give substance to the dream and make it come true—with the help of a great many other resourceful men of vision.

So we have some pretty good precedents for allowing the mind to reach out into the unknown and sort out relations or differences between fact and fantasy.

Sowing and Reaping

We see the rape of Belgium in World War I and remember unhappily how noncombatants and others were mutilated. Of what antecedent cause may this be the effect? What have they sown that they should reap such destiny? And we think of how, in the diamond mines of the Belgian Congo, native workers had suffered mutilations for real and/or fancied wrongdoings, from their Belgian masters. Suppose that the Belgians who mutilated the Congolese in the early days of Belgian domination had incarnated again by the time of the Great War, and as they had done to others, the same was done to them. "All who take the sword will perish by the sword" is the unequivocal statement of the Master Jesus. It does not often "seem" so. Most of those who take the sword do not perish by the sword; not, that is, in the same lifetime. But if one lifetime is not all of our sojourn on this earth, if we return, may not this be one way by which the Master's words are fulfilled?

"Think not that I have come to abolish the law and the prophets; I have come not to abolish them but to fulfill them. For truly, I say to you, till heaven and earth pass away, not an iota, not a dot, will pass from the law until all is accomplished." We have cited only one possible example of national karma. You, the reader, may sadly think of several others.

It is needless for us to beat ourself over the back by recalling painfully some of our own country's karma. *Karma is not all bad. Far from it.* It is both good and bad. We are reaping as we have sown. So as Dickens wrote of his own days, "It was the best of times, it was the worst of times, it was the age of wisdom, it was the age of foolishness, it was the epoch of belief, it was the epoch of incredulity, it was the season of Light, it was the season of Darkness, it was the spring of hope, it was the winter of despair."

These words have a relevancy for today as for the time of the French revolution about which Dickens was writing. Must things be ever thus? No, they must not. They need not be. But they will be as long as man returns evil for evil. "History repeats itself" because men set the pattern of repetition. As long as man perpetuates the law of retribution that Moses stated so long before the time of Jesus: "an eye for an eye; a tooth for a tooth."

When Jesus admonished His hearers to return good for evil, He was not only speaking as a master of compassion. He was telling them what everybody in the world of today, as of His own time, should know: that it is to everybody's advantage to temper justice—man's own concept of justice—with mercy. Man's tendency is to execute justice upon others, but want mercy for himself.

How to Find Freedom

The way of escape is the upward way.

There are intimations that men are beginning to learn this fact, even though strife, bloodshed, and inhumanity are still rampant in the world. We are finding that many men and some nations cannot sustain hatred for their erstwhile enemies for very long. This is good spiritual wisdom, and one can hope that some people at least see it as such; that it is financially profitable in some cases but casts a cloud of doubt over man's motivations. The *direction* is right, whatever makes him go that way.

No man is exempt from the action of natural and spiritual law. We can fight against it and maim ourself in the process, or we can work with it and reap a blessing.

Use or lose is the price of possession. Exercise your body, nourish it properly, keep it clean, and you are inviting health and physical well-being; neglect it, fail to appreciate it, and it becomes weaker and prey to all manner of afflictions. So with the mind. So with the emotions. So, too, with our freedoms.

Let a man appreciate, foster, and claim his freedoms and they become more strongly established. Let him fail to take part in local or national affairs, disregard the issues, fail to exercise his right to vote for leaders of his choice, and he is inviting someone, motivated by the lust for power, to take over.

People in many nations have waited too long, done too little and too late, before they have seen the handwriting on the wall, and as a result have become subject to dictators.

Greece, Rome, Babylon! Shall we extend the list to the painful present? What can we do? If we don't know what we can do, and do it, we could be already lost. "It is later than you think" was the motto on the wall of a garden in ancient China. Now even the wall is gone.

Many sense the fact that "the times are out of joint." But it isn't just the times. It is the defeatist attitude of individuals. Young people the world over sense that something is wrong. So far so good. But it would not seem that dissociating oneself from "the establishment" is going to help very much. Getting involved, which is much talked about but not done very effectively, is the young generation's prescription. Taking the prescription, acting on it, would seem more practical.

If someone sees smoke, it is a sign of fire. If he takes action toward putting the fire out, the house may be saved. If he simply walks away because he doesn't like smoke and fire, he may end up with no house and no place to go.

Thinking on these things, I often repeat to myself a meditation that I wrote years ago, but which has never appeared in book form:

"I'm grateful for the power which makes me do the thing I should, and ultimately, of my own free will; grateful for every lesson, which has shown me (when I could not, would not, see the right way and its blessings) the futility of every other way.

"Rebellion taught me wisdom's way, of working *with the law,* replacing condemnation and distrust by understanding.

"For want, the specter of the poor, I give my thanks, since it has shown me infinite supply. Strange that we should go to God only when all else fails—and yet 'tis Godlike too, for He would have us find His counterpart within, and rest on it, relying on ourself and our untried capacity.

"Through grief, that self-named virtue of bereavement, I've learned its other name, and it has stood revealed, disrobed, as selfishness. No more I mourn the loss of those beloved who loved me, because I've found my grief was for myself, not them. To grieve when progress calls them on were selfishness indeed.

"Pain taught me temperance, and respect for every power that God has given. In pain is wrapped the mystery of misuse, which righteousness (right use) redeems. And he alone who knows the pain can share the joys of life.

"I'm grateful for the loneliness which forced me to the truth that no one is alone, that all are one; and he who finds no comradeship within can never find it in another.

"And so for everything that life affords, for stormy days and shining skies, I'm grateful—and best proved so, not by what I say or write (for statements need their confirmation in our life), but by the thoughts which in my inmost mind I feel; by the serenity and poise I daily strive to win; by love I want to feel for everything that God has given life; by tolerance and mercy in the powers I wield; by humility in what I have achieved; by courage to look onward through the years, not blind to problems they will bring, but strong to face them. Thus may I prove *grateful*.

"This thing I know: As each day comes and goes, freighted with its weight of circumstances, I'll grow strong to meet the lessons it affords. The Source of Being which has brought me thus far on the path will not desert me now; and I best fit myself for His high service by doing gratefully and well the task that He assigns. I know that to be truly great consists . . . in part at least . . . in *being grateful*.

"And so to live the grateful life I try, and so I seek the good in everything. But most of all, when each day's work is done, and rosaries of gratitude are said, there still remain the faith and hope of days to come, and work to do, and strength to see it done. For these, oh, most of all . . . *I'm grateful.*"

Your Faith Is Your Fortune

"When everything else fails, read the directions," a housewife humorously advises would-be cooks and amateur mechanics.

This is practical advice in many areas, notably in a philosophy of life. Here are some very practical directions:

"If any of you lack wisdom, let him ask God who gives to all men generously and without reproaching, and it will be given him. But let him ask in faith, with no doubting, for he who doubts is like a wave of the sea that is driven and tossed by the wind," says James. Or in the words of Jesus, "Ask, and it will be given you; seek, and you will find; knock, and it will be opened to you."

No doubt you are familiar with Paul's famous dissertation on faith which begins: "Now faith is the assurance of things hoped for, the conviction of things not seen. For by it the men of old received divine approval." He then goes on to list eleven powerful examples of miracles wrought by faith. Jesus puts the whole matter in fewer words: "If you have faith as a grain of mustard seed, you will say to this mountain, 'Move hence to yonder place,' and it will move; and nothing will be impossible to you."

As in so many things that Jesus said, there is more to this statement than meets the eye. You have to follow the direction with understanding. For Jesus is talking about a very special kind of faith, special because it will

107

direct you to a tremendous discovery; a discovery that will enable you to dissolve—or surmount—mountainous difficulties and challenges.

Springtime Miracle

Let me quote from an article I once wrote for *Daily Word* magazine. It begins with a reference to a winsome little hillside house where I lived for years. Its largest window looked out over a sloping hill toward the sea. In fancy I can picture it now.

It is springtime, and I watch a miracle take place before my eyes from day to day.

The soft green of new growth is being transformed. The hillside is becoming a carpet of golden yellow, like part of the sun itself embodied.

The mustard is in bloom.

To crop gardeners the mustard is a pest.

To the early Catholic padres who dropped seeds as they journeyed from early mission to newer one, it formed a trail, *El Camino Real*, the Highway of the King.

To me it is a reminder of faith.

I never see the mustard come to bloom but what a picture from the life of Jesus comes vividly to my inner eye.

In Palestine the mustard grows to an astonishing height—tall enough, as one writer reminds us, to shelter a horse and rider from the sun.

All this from a tiny seed.

"If you have faith as a grain of mustard seed," the Master said.

What is faith "as a grain of mustard"?

There are many kinds of faith. Every man lives by

some kind of faith. If he only fears, he must have faith; for who can fear that in which he has no faith?

Every man has faith in something.

We write checks. We wind and set alarm clocks, or we push a plug into a socket, and expect electricity to run the clocks, and do a lot of other similar things.

We entrust our funds to people we've never seen to operate businesses we've only read about in magazines whose editors we've never met.

We entrust our very life to the mechanism of a high-powered car on a crowded freeway, and to the functioning of human hair-trigger mental reactions—our own and others'.

Yes, we all have faith in something.

And by faith—in many forms—I have seen the weak made strong, the sick made well, the lame made whole, the blind made to see. I have seen the impoverished become wealthy, enemies made friends, problems solved. All this by faith.

Such faith has been disparaged, but it has endured and has grown and spread long after its detractors, and the faithful too, have succumbed to "the last enemy."

Faith in People

There are many forms of faith. There is the faith we have in people. It can lead us to a greater faith, or it can discourage us if we become disillusioned about their powers or integrity.

An evangelist once came to a town where I lived, proclaiming the power to heal. A woman who had been blind for more than a score of years received her sight, beheld the face of her young son whom she had never seen. After the evangelist went on to another town, the woman's sight dimmed again to blindness. She evidently had faith in the power in the healer, but no faith in a like power in herself.

Jesus healed others. He inspired faith in them. Often their faith was faith in Him, not in what He taught them. When He was with them, their faith was strong. Often it subsided when He was gone. His presence was a stimulus to faith, but it was their faith in Him that alleviated their sufferings. For healing to be enduring, something very special is demanded of the individual himself. We cannot walk very far by a borrowed light.

There is faith in things: faith in charms, amulets, fortune-telling, mantras.

Perhaps you know the story of "Grandma's Boy." He was timid and shy. His grandmother gave him an ivory carving, to which she ascribed magical powers. It could, she assured him, give him courage, could enable him to do many wonderful things. And he did. Later he discovered that the ivory carving was only a discarded umbrella handle. By then he was able to believe that he could do wonderful things anyway.

There is a kind of faith that is a stimulus, as many medicines are stimuli. A medicine may alleviate a bodily condition. But unless the cause of the condition is reached, the trouble may recur. The man may be "cured," but he is not "made whole" unless the stimulus is sustained.

There is faith in prayer and God, which is a different order of faith because it is less concerned with establishing results than in recognizing causes.

"Your faith has made you well," said the Master on one occasion. Your faith!

Jesus had many things to say of faith. To me, perhaps, He was clearest of all in the parable of the mustard seed.

Mustard Seed Faith

What is mustard seed faith? Is it, as has been often assumed, a very small faith? Was the Master saying in effect, "If you have a faith as small as the tiny mustard seed, you can remove mountains"? Partly that. Surely that as a beginning. But though the mustard seed is not very large, there are others smaller to which the Master might have referred, if that were the point of the story. Why did He choose the mustard seed as an example of mighty faith?

Because the tiny seed becomes so great a plant! Because, too, the seed and the plant were so familiar to those to whom He was speaking. To them, as to me now, it was an impressive illustration of faith working from within the subject. The faith of the tiny seed is not a tiny faith, but a very large and productive one. It is faith to fulfill its own destiny.

Out of its hard little covering the germ of life in the seed bursts forth. Down through the dark it pushes a tiny shoot. Into the light and air it sends leaves and stem and branches. Soon it is a tall, wide-spreading plant.

It does not waste its energy trying to be a lily or a rose. It does not bemoan its lowly fate. It does not spurn its place in life. It grows where it has fallen, and faithfully outpictures the pattern that the Creator has put within it. The germ of its own pattern of fulfillment is born within it.

Outside forces can help—or hinder—it. Conditions

111

favorable or otherwise may affect its growth in degree; but unless it reaches out from within itself to fulfill its own life-pattern, it will not grow at all.

It is so with us.

Jesus was telling us that the pattern of our own fulfillment is within ourself.

"Whatever you ask in prayer, believe that you receive it and you will," is His assurance.

Power to Be—What?

"Whatever you ask." Does this mean that we can become anything we want to be? I think it means that our true desire is to be our own true self, in fullness and completeness. We can never be anything else. To try to is illusory, misleading.

As a boy of twenty I had a preceptor, teacher, spiritual advisor: John Walden, a man twice my age. He had faith in me and would not accept my own lack of faith in myself as being valid. He held before me always a vision of myself as "in dominion," capable, original, talented.

I did not share his faith. I had faith in him. Often he would have me share in devotional services with him. As he was talking to his listeners, I would sit in awe. He was so capable. He knew just the right word to use. His thoughts flowed freely and engagingly. He swayed an audience as few men I have known were able to do. I would be carried along in thought by the spell of his oratory.

Then would come the sickening, devastating thought: "I am too young, too timid, too ignorant. I can never be like him." I would silently pray that the chancel floor would open up and swallow me. I would think desperately of rising and rushing headlong from the public eye. Only my fear of failure, added, as it seemed to me, to many failures, deterred me. That, and his faith in me.

It took me five years to accept the idea that I could never be like John Walden. Indeed, as he would have been the first to assure me, I should not try to be. For better or worse I must be myself, the best self possible, but yet myself.

The turning point came when we were to conduct a series of services in a city new to us. As always he outlined the program, then showed it to me for approval. He had planned for both of us to speak at each meeting. For the first time in our association, I insisted on a change. "You take one meeting. Let me have another. Morning, afternoon, evening, it doesn't matter which."

He looked hurt. "You don't want to appear in the same service with me any longer," he said.

"It isn't that. I must find myself. I must find out what I have to say, whether people will listen, not because I am with you, but because I am me."

I have never become like John Walden except in what I have learned from him; never approached his eloquence, his engaging delivery. The mustard seed of me never became the impressive garden flower—and not even a very large mustard plant, but a mustard plant, nevertheless. To be less than that would be nothing; to be anything else would be pretense.

What is it that Emerson tells us? "A man should learn to detect and watch that gleam of light which flashes across the mind from within, more than the lustre of the firmament of bards and sages." There is much that others can do for us, but there is one thing that only we can do for ourself. We must "stir up the gift of God" that is within us.

God Works in You

Am I discounting faith in God? Quite the opposite. I am reminding you and myself that God's good for us must come through us. This is the great strength and power of Jesus. He knew the inward presence of God. "The Father in me does his works," He said. In everything, He turned to and worked with the aid of that inner presence.

In love and reverence we, if we are Christians, turn to Jesus. To whom did He turn? To God. And not to a God afar off, but within. He admonished us to do the same. "The kingdom of God is in the midst of you," He plainly said. The key words here are *God is within you*. Again He said, "Seek first his kingdom (which is within you) and his righteousness (the right use of the power this gives) and all these things (results that seem miraculous) shall be yours as well."

Frequently men seek that kingdom last. "The world is too much with us." "Things" clamor for attention. Our gaze, our attention, the focus of our interest, is inclined to be outward. We are impressed by what Paul spoke of as the "powers" and "principalities" of the world. Meanwhile heaven waits.

How shall we find, how shall we quicken the faith-to-become? By dwelling on the thought that all that we shall ever be, all that we are capable of becoming, already exists in us as an inherent pattern, a limitless potential, the divine *imprimatur*.

Your Fortune

Your faith is your fortune: your faith is the nature, the power, the presence of God within you. Of outer things, persons, conditions, circumstances, say with the Master, "What is that to you? Follow me!"

Let thoughts, feelings, words, actions take their motivation not from the outward world—as to the person unaware of his divine potential they are likely to do—but from mustard-seed faith, faith in the pattern God has established within you. One of the many allusions to this concept in Holy Writ is in one of the stories of Moses, referred to by Paul in his letter to the Hebrews: "When Moses was about to erect the tent, he was instructed by God, saying, 'see that you make every thing according to the pattern which was shown you on the mountain.' " The hidden meaning here is that the "tent" refers to the temple of man's indwelling—his body. "On the mountain" refers to the "secret place of the Most High," the place or state of communion within man where he receives inspiration from God within.

To activate this inner power and inspiration, affirm that nothing and no one can take or keep your good from you, that it came with you into the world, and that your faith in this heritage is the first step in its expression. Affirm the immanence as well as the transcendence of the nature of Christ. Dwell on Paul's words, "Christ (the nature of God) in you, your hope of glory."

Remember that He will not fail you or forsake you. God is never more than a thought away. In the moment that you consciously turn to Him and to His nature in you, lo, He is there.

Affirm: *"God works in me to will and to do whatever He wishes me to do, and God cannot fail.*

By a Waterfall

The story is told of a bird that built its nest on the branch of a tree overhanging a waterfall. The winds lashed the branch. Spray weighted it down. The nest seemed in continual danger of dislodgment. Yet the bird was undismayed. For its security was not in the branch, not in the nest, but in its wings.

Find your wings!

Do not compare yourself with others. Dwell not on what cannot be done but on what you can do. Respect your own powers and abilities. If you can only see a little way, go as far as you can see to go, even though humanly you may question the outcome. If you have not yet discerned the ability to do big things, do the little ones, boldly, confidently, in faith. Big things are seldom born big. They are born small, and they grow. Molecules are made of atoms. Beaches are made of sand, bodies of cells. Cities, states, and nations are composed of individuals. In a cosmos of ever-expanding horizons, in a time of the conquest of space, and man's growing awareness of infinity, the fission and fusion of atoms is seen to be the source of stupendous power.

Your own being is a center of power in the things of the world, and in things that are not of this world. Man is tapping the secrets of the universe. His greatest conquest remains the conquest and release of his own innate potential.

How Different Are We?

Most of us know what it is like to doubt, to be like a

wave of the sea that is driven and tossed by the wind. It always seems to us that our situation is unique, that it is different from the problems of other people, other times and places. In part this is true, because no two of us are exactly alike; but the problems we have are as much alike and as different as we are like other persons and different from them. It is one of the amazing "miracles" of human experience that the same essential truths can be relevant to so wide a variety of human experience.

The only thing that keeps people generally from knowing this is that they do not actually put it into practice in their lives. It seems so simple. It *is* simple, but it is not therefore invariably easy. It becomes easy, or easier, by practice.

To repeat: When everything else fails read—and let us add, follow—the instructions.

The instructions are simple. They are plain. You have read them, heard them, quoted them. Perhaps you have also applied them in your own experience, and thereby can quote them "as one having authority"—the authority of the actual experience.

No experience comes to us by chance; all appears in response to the universal law of action and reaction, the law of equivalence between consciousness and facts.

Meet Fact with Faith

We cannot wisely ignore the facts of human experience. It is better to meet them with faith. As Ervin Seale writes: "Sometimes confusion results when students are instructed to 'deny the facts.' You do not get rid of ugly facts by denying them. The facts in any situation are manifestations of the consciousness behind them. Thus, they are legitimate even if disagreeable. They cannot be denied or ignored, nor need they be. . . . Simply acknowledge that facts do not cause themselves; they are not causal. Thus you need not fear them. They cannot think, move, or act. On the other hand, consciousness alone is cause. Think of a better picture, a more suitable set of facts, and then know that the Word in you is causal and powerful and active. It is the only cause. Stand fast in this and know that a universal principle is at work for you. God is bringing new facts into being."

I thought of this as a man sat across from me recently to pour out his problems and seek relief. He has been unable to get work, payments are overdue on his car, he and his family are about to be evicted from the apartment in which they live. His wife thinks he is not trying hard enough, that he does not have the will to succeed. He has about decided that she is right; that she would be better off without him. He comes to me filled with doubt, doubt of himself, doubt of the power of prayer, doubt of the very existence of God.

Where to Begin

"I am glad to have you tell me about these things, but it is very hard to begin with negations and try to bring God into them. So let's begin at the other end of things, which means to begin at the beginning. Let's table the facts for the moment and get ourselves in a state of mind by which to deal with them intelligently. There's a prayer I'd like to have you say with me. I will say it, line by line, and ask you to repeat it with me:

I am a child of the living God.

I have within me the all-creating power of the Christ.

It radiates from me, and blesses all whom I contact.
It is my life, my strength, my courage,
My patience, my peace, my poise,
My power, my wisdom, my understanding.
My joy, my inspiration, and my abundant supply.
Unto this great Power I entrust all my problems,
Knowing they will be solved in love and justice.
Lord Christ, I've laid all my desires upon Thine altar,
And I rest in Thy graciousness."

He thanked me, and said he felt better.

"But it doesn't seem to be any kind of an answer to your needs. Is that what you're thinking?"

Somewhat shamefacedly, he admitted it.

"It never does at first. But keep repeating it, even if it seems to have no connection. Think about the meaning of the statements as you say them. You haven't been thinking of yourself as a child of the living God, have you? Nor that you have within you the all-creating power of the Christ? This concept has not been radiating from you and blessing all whom you contact.

"I'm not saying these things to criticize you. I am just giving you a kind of road map to use: a truth to know and a way to go, in your thought and feeling about God, yourself, other people, the human predicament. My prayers for you are nowhere near as effective *for you* as your own realization of this prayer will be in your life and world, as it helps you reorganize your inner world of thoughts, feelings, attitudes. There is no magic in the words, but when you accept the ideas they embody, they may well seem so. I've seen it work."

I handed him a pad of paper and a ball-point pen, and asked him to write down what we had affirmed together. I could have done it for him, or given him a typewritten copy, but I felt strongly that he would get more out of it, it would be more important to him, if he did it himself.

On radio and television, in the printed word of books and periodicals, before services and classes of hundreds and thousands, these truths that help us to deal intelligently with facts are expressed. Whenever they are actually put to work in human consciousness, they are effective. They were in the case just described. Because the man had a will to work at this as he had worked, and wanted again to work, in the commercial world.

"It Seemed Like a Miracle"

He did not lose his car. He was not evicted from his residence. He did get employment. His wife is as proud of him as if she had known all along that things would transpire successfully.

I could trace with you each step by which these results came about, just as they were reported to me. It was exciting to me to follow this man's progress. But though it is exciting to experience or to hear, it is dull reading, as most clinically detailed reports are. It is futile to recount the steps, the turns, the ups and downs, the disappointments and fulfillments, because they will never occur again in the same way. You or I can apply the same truths as did this man. We can attain comparable results; the outline will be similar; the fill-in will be as different as you and I or he and we are different.

The directions are many times stated in Holy Writ and elsewhere. There are other prayers of at least equal value and persuasion.

Find Your Answer

Here we have offered one set of direction, one procedure, one prayer, one outworking of God's law. Throughout this book, in almost every chapter, you will find other examples of the outworking. Somewhere among them you may find a situation that seems like one you have faced or are facing; or one that can encourage you to act upon a formula that has been tested and proved in real life. If you have already done this, you can bear witness to the truth; if not, you have before you along the way of attainment, the thrill of putting yourself in the picture. That is what we call "the Truth" is all about.

In Every Need, and in This . . .

It was in the last year of World War I, and I was a youth not yet of age, on a journey halfway across the country to reach a little town on the Gulf coast of Texas for my first assignment as a minister. It was a long journey, involving a couple of nights' effort to sleep in a stuffy upper berth of a stuffy Pullman car. It was hot (there was of course no air-conditioning in those days) and every time someone else or I wrestled one of the resistant car windows open during the heat of the day, clouds of smoke and cinders were added not only to the already well-supplied upholstery of the plush seats we sat on, but to our clothing, skin, and hair.

I began to feel ill the first day of the journey, but I already felt that I knew about psychology, suggestion, and homesickness, any one of which could weaken a youngster going alone into a part of the country strange to him, a career dependent upon the showing he might make in his first assignment as a minister. There was an influenza epidemic abroad in the land. On every station platform of towns that we passed could be seen piles of white boxes containing coffins. "Oh, psychology! Oh, suggestion! Oh, nostalgia! I know you all. I know there is no reason I should feel any different inside than I did in San Diego. I do not have to have a fever. My stomach doesn't have to be upset. It is only the cinder-laden smoke that gives me the sniffles. I am not going to start my ministry by coming down with the flu!"

123

So after climbing into my berth at night, I repeated over and over again *The Prayer of Faith:*

"God is my help in every need;
God does my every hunger feed;
God walks beside me, guides my way
Through every moment of the day.

I now am wise, I now am true,
Patient, kind, and loving, too.
All things I am, can do, and be,
Through Christ, the Truth that is in me.

God is my health, I can't be sick;
God is my strength, unfailing, quick;
God is my all, I know no fear,
Since God and love and Truth are here."

until it seemed to me that the click of the wheels over the rail connections caught the rhythm of my fevered words, and I drifted off into a troubled sleep. In the morning the sun was bright, the fever gone.

It was my first experience in applying *The Prayer of Faith* to a need of my own. The number of those who have found comfort, understanding, and physical healing through that little prayer is legion.

I have sat at the bedside of a youngster just old enough to talk, wracked with a fever greater than that early one of mine, smoothing the tousled hair from the flushed brow, and telling her that she was going to be all right, that God would make her all well again, and asking her to repeat after me the words of the prayer. In her childish treble she lisped them after me. Soon she fell asleep. The fever broke, and in a day or so she was

124

her lively, active self again.

After a Storm

During the years that I served as editor of Unity's magazine called *Youth*, I received a letter from the teacher at a school for girls on one of the islands in the Mediterranean. Some of her pupils went out in a small boat to greet a cruise ship coming slowly into port. There had been a storm the night before. The passengers were tossed about, and some of them reacted strongly to the violent motion of the ship. As morning came and the storm abated, passengers who had found their sea legs came out on deck. They were astonished to hear the melody of the hymn tune "Hursley" (commonly identified as "Sun of My Soul") sung with the words, "God is my help in every need," floating through the still air to them. It was the children from the school who had learned the song in English from the teacher who wrote me about it.

At almost the same time, a feature article appeared in the erstwhile American magazine, about a boys' school in the state of Washington. It was supported (and not too abundantly) by various charities and what work the older boys could do after school. One morning when they came to breakfast, food was in short supply. Their preceptor had taught the boys to pray, and now, he decided, the need for prayer was great. He asked them to close their eyes as they were seated about the table with him, and say with him *The Prayer of Faith*. While they were praying the sound of a truck was heard, followed by a rap at the door. It was a delivery truck, loaded with groceries.

But these stories seem almost trivial—if any answer

to prayer can be rightfully so described—compared to the story of a young man who was attracted to our Los Angeles ministry. I've told the story to *Weekly Unity* readers, but feel it will bear repetition here.

At My Open Door

With the feeling that someone was observing me, I looked up from where I was seated at my study desk, and there in the doorway stood as handsome a man as I've ever seen on the motion picture screen.

"May I help you?" I asked.

"I know you can," he responded.

Without knowing what his need might be, I too felt that I could help him, for the simple reason that a long time ago in the very beginning of my ministry, I had had a series of encounters with individuals with one special problem which baffled me. I couldn't seem to help. So I prayed earnestly to God, not to let anybody that I couldn't help come to me. Then I would know that if a person did reach me for counseling, I could be a channel of God's help for him. Did God answer and tell me that He endorsed this proposition? No, excepting that it has worked out, at least in degree, in the way I hoped.

The young man was an epileptic. He had had a seizure while alone at home, and finding himself without any funds at hand, had walked the couple of blocks from where he lived to the boulevard, and thumbed a ride to our church, which was just off the boulevard a couple of miles distant. He had attended some of our services, heard me on radio, and had the conviction (guidance?) that if he could reach me he would get help.

Our interview and prayer that afternoon marked the beginning of one of the most remarkable series of answered prayers in my years of ministry.

First there was the challenge of epilepsy, not so formidable to my thought as apparently to some other counselors. I have never accepted the concept that persons with this problem are more carnally-minded than "normal" people, or that they are sexually immoderate, as some authors and counselors have implied. In my somewhat limited experience I've found them to be supersensitive, with a tendency to try to repress their emotions, until finally an inner tension would build up and find release in a kind of nervous explosion, taking form in what is called *petit mal,* or less frequently but more violently, *grand mal.*

The First Step

Hugh's problem took the form of *petit mal.* We would begin counseling sessions with some relaxing affirmations, sitting comfortably opposite each other, following very much the kind of affirmations you will find in May Rowland's book *Dare to Believe!* In the chapter "Come Ye Apart Awhile" we come to this:

"As a first step in the practice of relaxation, we acknowledge one presence and one power—God, the good omnipotent. Then we quiet our thoughts and emotions by saying: *'Be still, and know that I am God.'*

"We think about God's love surrounding, infolding, and protecting us. We feel very close to God. We abide in the idea that 'underneath are the everlasting arms.' No evil shall befall us.

"Meditate on these ideas for a few moments, and you will feel a great sense of peace. Say to yourself: *'I*

127

relax in mind and body. I feel the peace of God. I rest in His loving presence.' "

It was months before Hugh's healing was complete. A major plateau was reached when he no longer had to resort to the use of a tranquilizer that a physician had described. It was a great day when finally that physician (with whom I had often cooperated) pronounced Hugh's cure complete, and for the first time in several years he was able to obtain a driver's license and experience the freedom of traveling on his own.

A Startling Call

I was startled one day, then, to receive a long-distance phone call from Hugh, originating in a city some fifteen hundred miles distant, and to hear Hugh's voice, not too vigorous, asking for prayers!

Hugh had always loved the out-of-doors, hunting, fishing, hiking. It was winter. He had been driving through a mountain area. The roads were slick and winding. His car had gone out of control, had gone over a steep bank, turned over and pinned him underneath. It was a full twenty-four hours before he was found. One of his legs had been pinned under the car, and he had been unable to free it. For a while it was thought he might lose the leg, then that it could be saved but that he would always be lame. Finally he was able to be released from the hospital and return home, hobbling courageously with the aid of a cane.

"Hugh, what were your thoughts as you lay there in the freezing cold, pinned beneath your car?" I asked him after our prayer together—thanking God for his life and limb.

"Intermittently I would pass out," he told me.

"When I was conscious I kept repeating the prayer you had taught me to say: *'God is my help in every need, and in this need.'* I was unconscious when somebody found me. They told me I was mumbling a prayer over and over, even then."

How he learned to walk without the cane, gradually with only the slightest suggestion of a limp; how he relinquished his boyish dream of a career in movies or television, for which he had little native talent, and instead established himself in a profitable business, married and became the father of a two-pound "pree-mie" who, with the help of Unity prayers, has become a stalwart young man, rivaling his father in size and appearance, is another story.

Guidance comes in many shapes and sizes. Hugh found it "accidentally" when, looking for something to help him pass a few minute's time one late afternoon, he came upon a variety program, and there, right in between Doctor Ross' Dog Food and the race results from Santa Anita, was a "Thought For the Day." "Funny place to discover a spiritual message," he remarked, "but it led me to the help I needed."

"It was where it should be for you, and maybe for a great many others who might not seek it out in a church. There it was right in the midst of everyday things that occupy most of people's waking hours."

Out of a Trash Can

I was delighted one Sunday morning to greet two newcomers to church: a retired banker and his wife, who lived in one of Southern California's most beautiful coastal towns. "How did you happen to find us?" I asked.

129

I was a little perturbed when with some embarrassment they confessed that they had found a copy of one of my earliest books in a trash can.

"What do you suppose one of my books was doing in a trash can!" I exclaimed.

"It must have been there by divine appointment," the banker's wife tactfully supplied. The happy association, the spiritual growth, the friendships that resulted from that unlikely start seemed to justify her comment.

Perhaps we could think of such happy outcomes as being the outward signs of an inward grace—expressive of a relationship between two worlds, the world of imagery and the world of manifestation; a relationship that is best cultivated by putting ourself into a state of receptivity. Often we are in no state of mind and emotion to invite or respond to guidance from on high.

The familiar axiom, "Your ship can only come in over calm seas," expresses one directive. Another is proclaimed in the story of a misbehaving little boy who got mud all over his Sunday-go-to-meeting clothes at a picnic and in that sorry state had the temerity to ask his mother for another helping of dessert. "Go clean yourself up," she commanded. "You're in no condition to ask anything from anybody."

The Best Conditioner

Prayer is the best conditioner for putting us in that state of grace which Ralph Waldo Trine described as being "in tune with the Infinite."

Some of the young people of today say that they do not like the word *prayer*, that prayer is a way of begging. They are right from their point of view, if that is

130

the way they feel when they pray. *But you never have to beg God for anything.* These young people, and maybe some older ones as well, may find through meditation, if not in prayer, the willingness of God. "Before they call I will answer, while they are yet speaking, I will hear," was the promise to Isaiah. Jesus said, in His prayer before the tomb of Lazarus, "Father, I thank thee that thou hast heard me. I knew that thou hearest me always, but I have said this on account of the people standing by," and on another occasion, assured His disciples, "Fear not, little flock, for it is your Father's good pleasure to give you the kingdom."

There are prayers of petition, there are prayers of thanksgiving, and there are prayers of realization; no doubt there are special needs for each of them. The church I served the longest was known as the Thankful Church because virtually every prayer uttered there began with thanks. But most of my own prayers are simply the recognition that I am always in the presence of God, the Creative Principle of Being. As Walter Rauschenbusch has so beautifully put it:

"In the castle of my soul
  Is a little postern gate,
  Whereat, when I enter,
  I am in the presence of God.
  In a moment, in the turning of a thought,
  I am where God is.
  When I enter into God
  All life has a meaning.
  Without asking I know;
  My desires are even now fulfilled.

My fever is gone
In the great quiet of God.
My troubles are but pebbles on the road,
My joys are like the everlasting hills;
So it is when I step through the gate of prayer
From time into eternity.
When I am in the consciousness of God
My fellow men are not far off and forgotten,
But strangely close and dear.
Those whom I love
Have a mystic value.
They shine as if a light were glowing within them.

So it is when my soul steps through the postern gate
Into the presence of God.
Big things become small, and small things become
    great.
The near becomes far, and the future is near.
The lowly and despised is shot through with glory."

Get into Condition

Whenever I feel a little bit down or impatient or resistant to the thing I know needs doing, and that with a little more gumption I could do, I know I am not praying enough; that is, I am not in a state of grace, or am "in no condition to ask anything of anybody," or to get the clear, unclouded sense of the Presence and Power that puts me in tune with the Infinite.

Somerset Maugham, in "The Razor's Edge," compares prayer to pushing the button that lights an electric lamp. The current is already there and available, waiting to be used. Pushing the button establishes the condition, makes the connection, by which the power is transmitted, comes through.

"I am the light of the world . . . ye are the light of the world . . . let your light shine . . . I of myself can do nothing . . . the Father who dwells within me does his works."

Adventures in Prosperity

"Thou preparest a table before me in the presence of mine enemies." God has set a bountiful table before us, as long as the world is long, as wide as the world is wide. He offers us all the riches of the world worthily to enjoy; all the bounties of nature, all the people, all the experiences by which we learn and teach and live and grow; all the music and art and science of the world, all the philosophies and religions, all the records of the past, written in wood and earth and rock and sea, and in the forms of birds and beasts and fish and man, all the wonders and mysteries and problems and revelations of the present, the wonders of outer space and the wonders of inner space, and the anticipation of things to come.

When I first realized that in the Shepherd's Psalm the scene does not suddenly change from the hillsides and valleys and streams of Palestine to a banquet hall, but that these are the table of the sheep—and of the shepherd too—it was like a revelation to me, and I wrote about it in Unity's greeting booklet *The Song of Life.*

Perhaps not even the Psalmist realized that God has spread before us all a vastly more bountiful table, from which all his children may find nourishment, not only for the body's needs but the soul's fulfillment even more.

The application of truth is variable, the principle always the same. The Psalmist interpreted the love and provision of God in terms of the agrarian life he lived.

Does it apply in the vastly more complex and swiftly-paced world of today? I think it does, from the humblest walks and simplest needs to the higher echelons of human involvement.

Blossoms for Easter

I am reminded of one of my own early experiences in the ministry. My first charge as a youth of twenty was in a city on the Gulf in Texas. I was called to a congregation that my first teacher had served twenty years before. I got there in the fall, and in speaking for the Busy Bee Workers who were seeking a project I suggested that they plant flower bulbs in pots, with the notion that it would be inspiring, when Eastertime arrived, to adorn the chancel of the church with flowers grown by members of the congregation.

The idea was, I think, a good one that might be tried again. But somehow it didn't work out right. For when, the week before Easter, I issued a call for the flowers to be brought in, they were a sorry lot, with tall gangly stems and meager adornment of flowers, mostly of a variety locally called hypocrites. At best they would have been more appropriate for Christmas, for they resembled poinsettias, except that they were smaller, and what appeared to be red blossoms were not separate from but a part of the green leaves.

On the day before Easter most of them had been brought in and I stood in the chancel surveying them. "It will take a lot of pink and purple crepe paper to eke out any semblance of a floral display," I thought, and as in the case of the orphanage (which incidentally happened much later) I heard someone rapping on the great front doors. Hastening to open them, I found a florist's delivery truck, laden with Easter lilies and rambler roses, the gift of a Magdalen who because of her unchurchly background preferred to remain anonymous. Indeed some members of the congregation might have been shocked to know that the impressive decorations were provided by a woman of dubious moral standards. But the flowers could not have been more beautiful—or more lovingly given, I'm sure—if they had come from our most saintly member! "It seemed like a miracle!"

Wheat for Coffee

From my files too comes the instance of a distinguished man in the import-export business, husband, as it happens, of a famous and popular novelist. He was representing a country whose principal export in the world market was coffee. The bountiful yield of that year glutted the market. Coffee overflowed the warehouses and wharves. There was talk of dumping it in fields and burning it.

What could he do to help the economy? He wrestled with the problem, pacing the floor of the living room. His wife had turned on the radio in anticipation of a musical program almost due on the air, and his attention was caught by the closing words of a news commentator, referring to the vast oversupply of wheat in our country.

"That's the answer!" he exclaimed. He began negotiations by which both countries profited in the exchange of commodities that each needed.

Somehow God's "abundant table most graciously supplies each earnest aspiration that hourly doth arise," as a familiar hymn assures us. Whatever our

137

sense of need may be, there is in God's divine economy a rich supply. But in evaluating need and supply we are likely to stop too soon.

"Is not life more than food, and the body more than clothing?" asked the great Teacher. We can be well-fed, well-clothed, well-housed, yet impoverished if we have not found inward peace, a sense of purpose and fulfillment, self-approval, and acceptance by our contemporaries.

How shall we find these? I think we have to get better acquainted with ourself. And to do this we need to take some time from the demands and activities of the workaday world in which we live. We may feel that we cannot do this, and truly it often seems as though we cannot. Yet life has a way of overriding our objections.

The Hidden Blessing

A man who is prominent in the entertainment field found himself marooned short of his destination by a strike that interrupted airplane service. At first he fretted and fumed about it. He railed at passenger agents who assured him that they would do what they could; but there was really nothing they could do at the time. Finally he surrendered to the situation. "I've been told time and again—and said I accepted the notion—that there is some good in every situation if we'll only look for it. I wonder what good I can find in this!"

He went to a hotel, engaged a room, disposed of his baggage, and wandered down a street adjacent to the hotel. He came to a park and found a bench from which he could look out over a tranquil valley. Something of its tranquility began to steal into his thoughts.

He had worked hard most of his life.

He had taken advantage of every situation, every human contact that he thought would advance his career, provide more richly for his family.

"I had always thought," he confided to me later, "that I loved people, and I guess I have. But I also discovered that I loved them most, not for themselves, but for what they could do for me; that without consciously realizing it, I had gotten in the habit of using people without much thought of the effect on them." (He hadn't heard the admonition: *love* people, *use* things.) "That was their concern, I claimed, not mine. By the time the strike was over, there were a lot more people waiting for space than there were seats available; and would you believe it, I actually relinquished mine for somebody I thought needed it worse than I did! I felt that in a curious way I gained something more valuable to me at that point than the time I lost."

Involuntary Step Upward

Even illness (though I don't recommend it) can on occasion serve a similar purpose.

I went to see a longtime friend who for the first time in many years was hospitalized. He had been in bed for a week. "I wish a fellow didn't have to be sick to be in the hospital," he said. "For the first time in years I've sort of gotten caught up on my thinking. I'm going to make several changes in my life's activities when I get out of here."

He did.

He stopped maintaining a house much larger than was needed. He simplified his social activities, many of which had been continued from habit long after the zest and interest in them had vanished. He resumed a long-rejected habit of attending church. The last time I saw him he looked as if a weight had fallen from his shoulders. He looked younger and happier.

Another friend of mine is a woman whose zeal belies her years. She tends to take on responsibilities not required by financial need, but perhaps from the need to feel needed. Then every so often she takes off in her compact car and heads for the seashore. "I go out and look at the ocean to get my sense of values adjusted," she asserts.

When I'm lecturing in strange cities I like (when I can) to go into quiet churches, regardless of denomination, for a time of silent prayer. In one that I visited I was greeted by a motto on the wall facing the entrance. It read, *"I come here to find myself."*

An interrupted journey, a hospital experience, a trip away from accustomed surroundings, to the seashore, the mountains, a quiet valley, the desert, any of these may serve the purpose of bringing us to ourself, to a new dimension of thought and activity, to the experience of the presence of God, and a wider awareness of the table that God has set before us.

By Divine Appointment

"In due season we shall reap, if we do not lose heart." Disappointments can become opportunities— opportunities to realize that God opens ways where there may seem to be none. In print there is only one letter's difference between the words *disappointment* and *His appointment*. In life and in time there may be more space than we think is essential to the discovery, and the recognition may not be as easy. Yet for most of

140

us, good often comes in unexpected, unforeseen ways. God is truly our supply, but He chooses His own channels. Answers come as if by divine appointment.

I was disappointed when illness and unemployment in the family made it necessary for me to interrupt my academic education and acquire some education of a different kind.

I went to work as an apprentice-artist with a company that made engravings for reproduction in print. It was eleven years later that I was offered a position as editor of a young people's magazine which used many illustrations. What I had learned by the interruption proved invaluable to me. Divine appointment?

At one point, years later, in establishing a new ministry, for a while the outgo was much larger than the income. One Monday morning my assistant minister and I were preparing a bank deposit. I had asked him to count the Sunday offering. (We were too new an organization even to have a treasurer at that time.)

"It doesn't seem like very much," he commented.

"No, but let's bless every cent of it." The mail carrier had just brought in the mail. That wasn't very much either. "Let's open the mail. There might be a dollar or two of radio offerings."

We did, and unlikely as it might seem, the last letter of the batch contained a check for $400, from someone we had never heard of before and have not heard from since; a woman who wrote that she had received an unexpected bequest and wanted to share it with a Unity ministry. In a Unity magazine, she was attracted by our name, and felt led to send her gift to us.

By divine appointment? We certainly felt that it was.

We got quite emotional about it, actually. It seemed like God's way of saying, "See, I have not forgotten you." We offered a prayer of thanks to Him and to His channel of blessing to us. The gift seemed to mark a turning point in our ministry. Attendance and offerings both increased. Soon we were thinking in terms of our own permanent church home. We used the affirmative prayer: *This is God's work. It is divinely planned, divinely prospered, divinely sustained, divinely fulfilled.* The way in which this prayer was fulfilled, in wartime, when many people thought the area was likely to be bombed or invaded, is a drama in itself.

Follow Guidance

It was impossible to build. We had outgrown rented quarters and were looking for larger ones. Instead of renting we found a church building we could buy. It wasn't large enough. We found that a balcony could be added, if we could get the structural steel needed. Miraculously it was found. Following a hunch, we had it delivered even before the contractor was ready for it. That very night at midnight an embargo on deliveries went into effect. If it had not actually been in the building we could not have gotten it for three years.

The contractor, too, came to us by divine appointment. He had done some cabinet work for us. We learned that he had done major construction work, and asked his help. He had never heard of Unity before, but he had faith in our project. No contract was ever signed. It was a "gentlemen's agreement." The work proceeded with complete agreement and good will.

And the building we had contracted to pay for in twenty years was paid for in less than two—without a building campaign. People have called it a miracle.

Now I am convinced that in things both small and large, all that we do, the decisions we make, the places we go, the places we stay, the people we meet should be—indeed *are,* if we but know it—by divine appointment.

Interruptions

Are you bothered by interruptions? Try a paraphrase of a familiar Bible passage. Affirm *"No man cometh unto me save by the Father."* If someone reaches you then, look for something helpful he may say or do that will reveal a divine appointment in the experience.

Does someone demand help that you feel unequipped to give? The Father knows the need. Ask Him to direct each person to his own channel of fulfillment. Affirm your own oneness with God's purposes; that in whatever guise you serve, you are actually in His service. By the same token, then, He will not bring anyone to you for help unless you can be a channel. Again, *"No man cometh unto me save by the Father."*

If you have a trip to make, and there are apparent delays or frustrations, affirm: *"The spirit of the Lord goes before me, and opens ways, or guides me in paths, where there seem to be none. I stay and I wait and I move as by divine appointment. What the Father wills He also fulfills."*

If you face a challenge or a disappointment, do not let it disturb the calm peace of your soul. Affirm: *"This is the Lord's doing; it is marvelous in my eyes. Either the good as I see it, or what in His sight is even better, shall become manifest, without haste or delay, in per-*

fect ways and under grace."

"The eternal God is your dwelling place, and underneath are the everlasting arms," declared Moses.

Prosperity is basically an attitude of thought and feeling, only secondarily a matter of money. For ideas s are coin of the mind realm. This may sound like rationalizing to a reader who happens to be experiencing a financial stringency. (When I made such a statement in a study class one time, a member of the class challenged me: "It's all very well for you to say that. You don't know what it is to be without money, not to know where the next meal is coming from." I let her have her say before I responded: "Those assertions about me are a fine prosperity treatment. I am glad that you think of me in that way. Please keep on doing so. But as a matter of fact, I have come through some such experiences as you describe, and it was this teaching that brought me out of it!")

Enough and to Spare

A wealthy friend of mine attests to this. "My first job got me only six dollars a week. When it was increased to eight, I began to get the true idea of what prosperity means. That raise was a 33 1/3 per cent increase. Thinking of it in terms of the percentage of increase made me feel a lot better than thinking about the actual sum, two dollars. Actually it isn't how much money you make but how your needs are met that is the really important thing. You can be poor with a million-dollar estate if you *feel* poor; and I've known what it was to feel rich when I had so little money it didn't seem worthwhile to put it in a checking account."

This man stated the true principle of riches. Whether we realize it or not, we all live by what might be called invisible means of support.

The Law of Attraction

I was made to realize this graphically when I was called to Unity headquarters years ago to accept an editorship. For the first time in over ten years of ministry I was to work for a definite salary. I talked the matter over with Lowell Fillmore. He recommended that I should think of my salary as only one token of God's infinite supply; that He had many ways of augmenting my income. I worked out a prayer thought something like this: *God is my instant, constant, and abundant supply of all good. I am an irresistible magnet to attract the good that God has for me. I give rich service and am abundantly recompensed. I give where giving is needed. The return comes to me through God's divinely appointed channels. I strive to be worthy of the good I seek, and I leave the ways with Him.*

It worked; and the way it worked was that I was called on to teach classes at Unity, to speak for various civic organizations, and people who had asked for prayers began sending in belated tokens of their appreciation. So I was moved to say, as if I were joking but actually with reverence: *"I live by invisible means of support. I invest my energies in service, and God supplies the recompense. I do my work. He chooses the channels through which His blessings come."* Some of them I can anticipate, but He often surprises me. I make no law for myself about this. Imelda Shanklin, author of *What Are You?* used to say: "Don't say that your good must come from certain persons or projects.

145

Agree that it can come through both expected and unexpected ways."

Infinite Resources

Back of all the activities that we identify with prosperity, healing, good will, right adjustment, and happy outcomes are the infinite resources of infinite Being.

The wonders of this world in which we live are a part of our "means of support." We haven't earned them, at least in any identifiable way. They are part of God's free gifts to us (God's law of grace) to use, to share, to rejoice in.

I try to be mindful of these blessings. I thank God for them every day. But just in case I might be inclined to take them for granted, I turn now and again to Martha Smock's book *Meet It with Faith,* or the little book "Man Does Not Stand Alone," by W. Cressy Morrison, whom I've quoted in the first chapter. Each in its own way testifies to the fact that we actually do live by invisible means of support.

"In the morning sow your seed, and at evening withhold not your hand; for you do not know which will prosper, this or that, or whether both alike will be good."

"I am the Lord your God,
   who teaches you to profit,
   who leads you in the way you should go."

Over and over, throughout the Old and New Testaments, we are shown the pattern of prosperity. As you sow so shall you reap; as you give so shall you receive: to withhold the giving of our self, our services, our abilities, is conducive to lack; if freely we give, freely also we shall receive.

146

The giving comes first.

In the Way of Abundance

We cannot get another breath until we release the breath we have. The widow and her mite, the hunchbacked juggler performing before the statue of the Virgin, Demosthenes addressing the waves of the sea with pebbles in his mouth, the sower sowing the seed, the fisherman casting out his nets, Peter addressing the lame man at the gate of the temple called Beautiful: "I have no silver and gold, but I give you what I have; in the name of Jesus Christ of Nazareth, walk." These and a thousand other instances command us to put ourself in the way of abundance, by obedience to prosperity's first law, giving.

God feeds the sparrows, but He doesn't put the food in their nests.

Always there is something to do, something to give, if it is only our attention, our prayer, our devotion. Agree that there is something you can give, clear the stream of your thought and feeling—oh, especially your feeling—so that the stream of abundance pours out to bless you.

The beginning and ending of every story of "demonstration" is always the same: "in the heart of man, a cry; from the heart of God, supply." The details from first to last are always different, so that it is ever a new story yet ever the same. Ever new because it is new to you, and because you are you and not someone else; ever the same because the principle is unvarying. "Give and you shall receive."

Prosperity's second law, the law of receiving, would (you might think) almost take care of itself; and it does almost, with just a little help from you.

A Fine Art

Being a good receiver is something that cannot be taken for granted. It is a fine art.

To whom do you most enjoy giving? Obviously to a good receiver. Giving may be a duty, it may be a compliance with principle, but it is a good receiver who makes giving a joy. When someone's face lights up, when lines of anxiety and care disappear, when someone recognizes the worth of a service you render, a compliment you give, a present you proffer, you have already received abundantly—but you shall receive more.

Do not limit your notion of receiving to the thought that the return for your giving must come from the direction or the person to whom you give. Affirm: *"I give as I would receive, richly, freely, abundantly, joyously, promptly, as I would receive. There are no strings attached to my gifts. I am not trying to bargain with God or man. I give because it is God's spirit within me that prompts the giving. I leave the results for Him to determine."*

In the natural order, the return for our giving—as wages, fixed charges, and similar income—accrues from anticipated channels; but as many of the instances related in this book and countless others will attest, some of the most blessed returns that ever come to us come as from a higher law "out of the blue" as people often say; emphasized to our attention and evaluation because they are often so surprising and delightful.

Make Way for Your Good

Nature abhors a vacuum. Giving creates one. Give

the best gifts certainly, as you would wish to receive the best. But also make way for greater abundance in your life, by giving away whatever you do not have a use for. Such things, retained, block channels of supply. Let there be no "bags in your attic."

"Behold, I will cause breath to enter you, and you shall live." It must be apparent that prosperity's double law of giving and receiving is also the principle of good circulation. In the physical body good circulation produces prosperity of the body, as health. In the commercial world, good circulation produces the prosperity that we call financial affluence. "When things get tight, something has to give." When things get tight financially, *someone* has to give! We have to find some way to improve circulation.

One version of this concept can be applied to persons seeking employment. Oddly enough being out of employment—out of circulation really— is something that most persons experience perhaps only a few times in their adult life, if at all. Consequently, they are less well-prepared to find a job than to fill it.

The answer is: Take your sense of need out of isolation.

If You Want Work

Begin with an affirmative prayer something like this: *"God is my employer. I have a work to do, a place to fill, joys and bounties to be received and shared and given again, in a way that is unique, because I am unique; there is no one else exactly like me in all the world. My work awaits me. My good is seeking me even as I am seeking it. I go forth with confidence. I set God before me to prepare the way, and He opens ways*

149

where to my human sense there may appear to be none. 'I do a wonderful work in a wonderful way, I give wonderful service for wonderful pay.' I give thanks now that I have a job to do right now, the job of finding my rightful place of service, and preparing to fill it."

I once used almost exactly this concept, carried over into a somewhat unusual method of action in the case of a youth who came to counsel with me. His father was a skilled mechanic, employed by a reputable firm, but unable to collect his salary because of a (hopefully temporary) financial stringency. So the youth felt he must leave school for a time and get a job. He had tried without success when he came to see me. Finally, after some conversation and prayer, I said:

"I'll tell you what! How would you like to work for me?"

"Oh, that would be great! What do I have to do?"

"Well, you are to work daily, Monday through Friday, from eight in the morning till five in the afternoon, with an hour off for lunch, except on Wednesdays when you will knock off work at one o'clock. I will pay you a modest salary. And you are to report every day when you quit work, just what you have done through the day."

"Yes, but what do you want me to do?"

"Remember now: you have a job. You are no longer out of work. What I am paying you for is to find a job for a fine young man like you."

He found a job the first week.

What I Told Polly

Situated in Hollywood, I frequently had motion and television people come, seeking help in finding employ-

150

ment. Most of them were character actors, status-conscious, fearful of being too long "at liberty." My advice to them was invariably what in an earlier day I had told Polly Kelly, a red-haired businesswoman who was stranded in a small community when I first knew her.

Polly had had a very successful eating place in a large oil-producing area of Texas, when suddenly the wells closed down and she found herself living in what was almost a ghost town. She felt attracted to San Diego for some reason that I have now forgotten, and asked me to pray with and for her to find work.

"All right," I agreed, "if you will pray with me, and promise to follow the guidance you receive." Our prayer was very much like the one I have quoted. For a few days nothing happened outwardly. Then one day she phoned me from the hotel whose roon rent was rapidly using up her meager funds.

A curious thing had happened. Restless, she had strolled into the lobby of the hotel and fallen into conversation with a somewhat seedy-looking man who was back of the counter where cigars and souvenirs were offered for sale.

"You don't have much business," she ventured.

"No, business has gone to pieces," he agreed.

"No wonder, the way your stand looks! Dusty shelves. Grimy glass on the display cases. I have nothing to do for the moment. Let me help you straighten things up. No charge, you understand."

He accepted the offer joyfully, and soon the shelves and glass were gleaming, the stock dusted and rearranged. The next thing that happened was that he offered her a job, at a very small salary-about what I

151

had paid the young man for working at finding a job.

Polly called me up to report.

"That's great," I responded enthusiastically.

"You mean I should take it?" she exclaimed. "Is that the kind of God you have, offering me a measly job like that?"

"Well, you asked for His help. You promised you would follow His guidance. You wanted a job. Here is a job. Take it, and bless it!"

With considerable misgivings, and a sense of humiliation, she did. It wasn't long after that a customer began talking with her. "What is a woman like you doing in a place like this?" he said, or words to that effect. She mumbled an explanation that it was "better than nothing," without committing herself to how much better.

"I happen to know that the big hotel down the street is opening a lower-floor cafeteria. They're looking for a manager. With the background of experience you have, I bet you're just the one for it. Let me call up and tell them about you."

"Do you know somebody there?" Polly asked.

"No, but I feel like I know you. I know they need somebody like you. Maybe I can help put the need and the supply together. It's a hobby of mine."

He did, and she was invited for an interview, and got the job.

To Them that Have

People do not always like the advice I give. They say they will lose status, or that the work is beneath them. My thought is that it is always easier to get work when you have work, hard when you do not. Almost always I have found in the case of show-business people, that if they will accept some kind of work, the first that comes after prayer, it will lead to other and bigger offers. It might be surprising, though unfair, if I could tell you the names of some of these famous and near-famous people.

Put yourself in the stream of activity. Don't be a wallflower, a spectator, a left-over. Put your sense of need, and the talents and potentials you have to offer, into circulation, even if you have to offer to work for nothing. An obscure writer found himself out of work years ago. He couldn't seem to make a connection with any newspaper, at a time when reporting was his background of experience. Unhappy with inactivity, he tried writing a series of newspaper columns. He offered them to the leading newspapers. They all came back. Resentful, he offered them to small-town papers, at fifty cents apiece. He got several responses. The number grew from week to week, until one of the great newspaper chains hired him at a top salary, and syndicated his column. He became famous. He got himself into circulation. With quite a bit of help, you say? Yes, but help comes most abundantly when you make the first move yourself.

"I Sat Where They Sat"

Of all the possible guidelines toward trying to understand and improve the human condition, there are two that are essential, and a third that is the outgrowth of the two.

They are *a sense of values, a sense of direction,* and a resultant question, *what can be done about it?* In an effort to help other people work out a pattern of behavior that they can live with, and in an effort to find one of our own, these are paramount.

How well the Great Teacher understood human nature and human problems! "Do not lay up for yourselves treasures on earth, where moth and rust consume and where thieves break in and steal, but lay up for yourselves treasures in heaven, where neither moth nor rust consumes and where thieves do not break in and steal. For where your treasure is, there will your heart be also."

Where your treasure is! How little we seem to know ourself, or where our treasure is! To this day a certain mother of my acquaintance does not realize how she virtually pushed her young son, whom she adored, out of the house; and all over an old double bed. The room assigned to her college-age son was rather small, even with only a single bed, a desk, and chair in it. But there was stored in the garage a cherished double bed on which probably the young man had been conceived. The mother feared that it would become warped in storage (she and her husband had long since converted

155

to twin beds), and so it must replace the single bed in the son's room, which left him hardly room to change his clothes—but did cause him to change his abode. He found a more comfortable room in the home of a friend. Maybe she would have lost her son anyway, but was it not ironic that she should virtually but unwittingly push him out, and then bewail the fact that he had left her? Wrong on all three counts: no sense of values, no sense of direction, and certainly other things could have been done about it.

Transient Love or Enduring?

A husband and wife come to me for counseling. They don't like the same kind of house to live in, or the same kind of car to drive; her friends and his friends are not compatible. As a physician friend of mine described another couple, "He liked coffee, she liked tea, so they compromised by drinking cocoa which neither of them enjoyed." They don't have the same sense of values, nor the same sense of direction. I suggested something that often brings hidden factors to light—not a divorce but a trial separation.

Soon the husband was back to see me. He couldn't live without his wife, even though he couldn't live—at least amicably—with her. There was a strong sexual attraction between them which they had at first mistaken for love, a more tender bond. It was apparently the only thing they shared in common. What could be done about it? I didn't think I could help them preserve a nonexistent marriage, and felt that they needed a more specialized kind of counseling. I gave them the name of a reputable psychoanalyst. Was their sense of values, their sense of direction, enough to sustain a marriage?

Eric Fromm, the renowned psychoanalyst, writes: "Immature love says, 'I love you because I need you.' Mature love says, 'I need you because I love you.' " And further, "Most people are easily misled to conclude they love each other when they want each other physically. Love *can* inspire the wish for physical union, and when it does, the physical relationship is blended with tenderness. If the desire for physical union is not stimulated by love, it never leads to union in more than a transitory sense."

I suspect that this was one of my least satisfactory counseling experiences.

About to Commit Suicide

I receive a letter from a young man, well-known to me, serving his stint in the military service. He tells me he is contemplating suicide; that rather than take the life of a man he has never even been introduced to, he is going to take his own.

How do you appeal to such a youth against such a course? Yes, I know there is a theory that persons who tell you they are going to take their own life do not really intend doing it; that it is only a bid for attention and sympathy. I acted upon that theory once with another man, a man who was disappointed in love, and later I was called to officiate at his funeral!

So I was inclined to discount that theory, and did a lot of praying for guidance as to what I should write in response to this man's declaration. Finally in meditation the thought came to me that we are all giving our lives to or for something, often to such puerile things as seem not to justify all the wisdom, patience, growth, and intelligence that God and nature together have expended to produce the human species down through what James Freeman has called "the incredible centuries."

Here was a youth with a great potential, willing to "lay down his life" for an ideal. Was there not some way he could give it to greater effect?

Often with me, guidance will come in the form of a Scriptural passage. It was so in this case. The passage was from Luke: "Do not be anxious how or what you are to answer or what you are to say; for the Holy Spirit will teach you in that very hour what you ought to say."

With that I responded, "Thank You, Father," and started a letter to the boy. It went much like this:

"Dear John:

"Bless you for sharing your intimate thoughts and feelings with me. I sympathize with your resistance to taking the life of men with whom you have no personal differences, men with hopes and fears, dreams and despairs very much like your own. I think I would shrink from this with all my heart, but I don't think I am as brave as you. I have faced one or two experiences that made me think of suicide. I suppose most of us who have reached mature years have considered this. But each time I thought of it, I came up against this counter-argument:

"I am strongly convinced that life continues after death. I don't think we suddenly become transmogrified simply by relinquishing the physical body. I believe it is like going to sleep at night and waking in the morning. Maybe I am glad to fall asleep and forget for a while some challenge that confronted me through the day. But I find that in the morning I still have to face whatever lies ahead. And if I were to destroy my body, I suspect that I would still have to face whatever it was that motivated my self-destruction, and that meeting the issue might be harder out of the body than in it.

"So I offer this suggestion: If you are willing to give your life for an ideal, give it in a way that will mean the most possible good. Dedicate whatever time is allotted to you in this plane of life to serving God wherever you are.

"Say, *'Here I am, God. I did not consciously ask to be where I am, but I have to have faith that it is serving some good purpose, to learn and to grow, to overcome some weakness, to affirm some strength. So, I place my life in Your service, to do with as You will. If I am to continue in this world, let it be by Your decree; if not, that also by Your decree, not mine.'*"

It was nearly two months before I heard from John. His letter told me he had followed my suggestion. As a result, or by the kind of coincidence that seems like a miracle, he was placed in the medical corps, where his assignment was to help rescue the wounded and get them to a field hospital.

In due time he returned home and came to see me. "You saved my life, Doctor," he said. "Now I want you to help me fulfill it."

"What can I do to help you fulfill your life, John?" I asked.

"I've found the girl I want to marry. Will you

officiate?"

"Just tell me when!"

He did, and I did.

He had had a good sense of values, but without a sense of direction or of what could be done in a constructive way.

Why Am I Here?

A woman sits down in the visitor's chair, carefully places her handbag and gloves on the corner of my desk, attempts to pull her skirt down to her knees. She looks across at me, and I at her, in the moment of mutual appraisal that seems to be a part of every initial consultation. "Why am I here? Can I share my problem with this man?" I can picture her thinking.

I used to have this same sort of questioning: "Why is this person here? What, if anything, can I do to help?" But I no longer have this problem. I solved it—to my own comfort— by a prayer I've so often said that it is almost automatic with me: "O God, there are so many counselors a person in trouble can turn to! Don't let anyone reach me unless there is something I can say or do that will help. Then when someone *does* come to me, I will accept his coming as an assurance that he is here by divine appointment, and I will do my best to fulfill Your confidence in me." God has never told me in so many words that He agrees to this compact I offered Him, but I try to act as if He has done so, and somehow it helps me.

So, I think smilingly, as I did on this occasion, and ask with confidence, "What can I do for you?"

What she told me aroused my curiosity. She had, it appeared, been a waitress for twenty years. Until recently she had always had a job; one job after another, and in increasingly favorable surroundings, with increasing pay, and generally increased tips. Now, for the first time in her life, she couldn't get a job.

Had she been dismissed because she had been inefficient? Uncooperative? Hadn't gotten along with other employees, customers, her various employers?

She was an attractive-appearing woman, dark, slender, neatly dressed. In a kind of work in which there seemed always to be a demand for capable people, it was difficult to see why over a period of several months she couldn't get a job.

The answers were inconclusive, somewhat defensive perhaps, but no more so than usual.

I wasn't getting anywhere.

"All right. Fine. Let's have a little prayer together."

So I suggested relaxation, took a deep breath to fortify the suggestion, closed my eyes, and worded a somewhat lengthy prayer thanking God for His love, His bounty and blessing, His guidance in establishing right action and fulfillment for us both.

Finally I opened my eyes, and following an intuitive feeling that came with my "Amen," I said, without preamble, "Tell me, who is the matter with you?"

Whether it was the prayer, or the question, or a combination of both, I don't know, but it was as if I had touched a very sensitive nerve. Her eyes filled with tears, and she wept, sobbing. I sat quietly and let her cry because I know crying can often be therapy.

I shouldn't have been surprised, either, because it is usually a *who* rather than a *what* that troubles most any of us—and usually I don't have to ask the question.

When her sobs subsided I reached to the bottom lefthand drawer of my desk and pulled out some facial tissues, and pushed the wastebasket closer to receive them.

Then she began to pour out her story. It was indeed a *who*—a married man with whom she had become infatuated. Apparently he returned her affection. He would get a divorce. They would be married. But always there was something to delay the divorce. His wife was ill. Telling her would be cruel. He had to go on a sudden business trip. Or a son was being proposed for a fraternity. It seemed always a right time for her, never for him.

"Tell me," I said again, "if this man were to get a divorce, do you think he would want to continue the relationship with you? Would he then want to marry you?"

She lifted her eyes to mine, a look of surprise on her face, as if she were seeing something for the first time. "No, I don't believe he would!"

"Then what future do you think there is for you in the association?" I asked.

"Why, there isn't any, is there!" she exclaimed.

Subconsciously, I think, this woman had a good sense of values, and needed only to have the right questions put to her directly, to find a sense of direction, and the answer that she could live with.

Indeed, I think that the persons with whom I counsel mostly bring the solutions to their problems with them—solutions in some cases unrecognized, out of focus, or even rejected. I am mostly the listener and/or the interrogator. I simply help those who talk with me

162

to identify the problem, and often in simply doing so, reveal the cause and possible solutions for the problem. Often there is more than one answer. The one who has the problem must choose the answer he thinks he can best live with.

In Disguise

Sometimes too the problem is in disguise. A man sought some time with me. He was obviously accustomed to manual labor. His hands were gnarled and work-stained. His clothing was that of a workman. His story was one that I have heard, with variations, many times since, but it was new and incredible to me at the time—because I did not then know the depth of some human needs as to some degree I do now. He was, he told me earnestly, beset by hidden enemies, evil forces that worked against him. They caused him to lose one job after another. They interfered with his mail, and even opened and resealed letters before the letters reached him. These same forces inspired children in the neighborhood to call him names, to play boisterously outside the windows of his room, disturbing his rest.

What, I wondered aloud, could explain such persecution? It was, he confided, the work of a vast and powerful church organization.

"You must, then," I responded, "be a very important person, to merit so much attention, even though adverse, from so powerful an agency!"

"Oh, no! I am a very humble person. I clean offices at night. Look! Look at my hands. See how worn and calloused they are."

I shook my head. "You may appear so in your own sight, but I know better. It must be a clever disguise."

"Why do you say that?" he demanded.

I responded with another question. "Do you think I am important, my friend?"

"Oh, yes! You are the minister of a great church. You talk to people on radio and television. You are very important. That is why I have come to you for help."

"Then listen carefully. I am not important enough for this religious hierarchy that you say is persecuting you to pay any attention to me at all."

"I never thought of it like that," he said, with what sounded like disappointment in his voice.

There was a need for him to feel important.

There is a need for everyone to feel important.

When he failed to find a sense of importance in his humdrum world of drudgery, fantasy had supplied what fact denied this man.

I could not terminate the interview at that point or even with one visit. For I had taken something out of that man's life, which even though false, was better than nothing.

Could I offer him something in its place? I must try.

I remembered the instance of a judge who had sentenced a drug addict to a course of treatment that broke the habit. But in a short time she was brought before him again.

He reproached her sadly for not having kept faith with him.

"Judge, you took something out of my life. You didn't put anything in to replace it," she cried.

I felt that way about my cleaning man. He had risen to leave with a mumbled word of thanks.

"No, don't go yet," I asked him. "Come and sit down opposite me. There is something very important I want to tell you. And that is that *you are important.* I do not see it as you do, that there is an evil force working against you. The most evil force that can work against you is that you do not think you and the work you do are important.

"You, I, all of us, are important in God's sight, but we are important in the human scheme of things as well.

"Do you like music? Have you ever listened to and watched a big orchestra?"

Oh, yes, he had. On television. In the Hollywood Bowl, too.

"Somewhere, in that assemblage of a hundred musicians, there is one who seems to have little or nothing to do. Look for him and you are likely to find him sitting with a triangle in one hand, a mallet in the other, his eyes possibly staring at the music sheet on the stand before him. You cannot see it, but he is counting—maybe thirty-two or sixty-four measures of the music, while the violins and clarinets and other instruments are playing—just so at the very right moment he may go *Ding!* on that triangle.

"It is a nothing, or nearly nothing, you might say; yet it is very important that he come in at just the right time, neither too soon, or too late, or not at all.

"Maybe what you do is mostly unnoticed, because you do it so well. But if it were not done well or not done at all, it would be greatly missed. And you, because you are important to yourself, and to your employer, and most of all maybe to someone you love or

165

who loves you, must respect yourself and the work you do.

"You are as important in your field of effort as you think I am in mine. As long as you are a cleaning man, be the very best cleaning man there is, and keep knowing all the time that you are not just a cleaning man. You are an honest workman doing an honest job. And you are a child of God.

"You are as important to me as any person who comes to see me. You are important in God's sight. Know this. Say it over and over to yourself. This will free you from the troubles you came to see me about. Don't ever forget what I have told you, but if you do forget, come to see me again, and I will tell you again that you are—(I thought of Chico in the play "Seventh Heaven") 'a very important fellow.' "

Keep Showable

One evening an unprepossessing man, along with his mother who spoke only Hebrew, appeared at the door of my home. He had seen me on television and thought maybe I could help him. He was lonely, the girls would have nothing to do with him. All this was due to the fact that he had a very prominent nose. Tears came into his eyes and rolled down his cheeks as he poured out his sense of self-pity and rejection. His mother sat opposite us and wept in sympathy, intoning something that sounded to me like *"Oi, weh ist mir!"* Almost involuntarily I reached for the facial tissues and supplied them both.

I looked the young man over. His skin was oily and not too clean, his hair unkempt, his fingernails dirty, his clothes unpressed, his shoes needed shining.

"I'll tell you what," I said. "Give yourself a good scrubbing with plenty of soapsuds. Shampoo your hair. Get your clothes pressed, your shoes shined. Get a haircut and manicure. Make the most and best of yourself. Don't slouch when you're sitting, as I see you now. Stand tall when you are standing. I don't believe that that large nose of yours, other things considered, is too much in the way. I read a few days ago that Jimmie Durante has just gotten married to a pretty, blonde young woman. Turn sideways. Let me get a look at your nose in profile. I don't believe it is as big as his, and his hasn't been a handicap to him.

"We will have a prayer now. Then you do the things I've recommended. I am confident they will help solve your problem. If not let me know and I will help you find a surgeon who specializes in correcting facial defects."

We had a prayer. He left saying, *"Shalom!"* And I've heard from the man several times at holidays. He always signs his greetings, "Your Hebe Friend."

A Matter of Minority

There have been other instances of a similar nature. People who have some physical handicap that they feel sets them apart, people who are self-conscious about being members of a racial or religious minority. They do not realize that each of us is in some respect a minority of one. It is true that some of these things that "set us apart" are more obvious than others, and even unescapable, like a person's skin coloring. If you are Caucasian in the Western world you don't know what it is like to be *white* in the Orient, or in Nubian Africa!

"You don't know what it is like to be a member of a

167

minority, the embarrassment and misconceptions and rejections that this can mean!" a black man says to me.

True, I am a Caucasian, and do not experience what it must mean to belong to a racial minority. And I remember reading the account of a white man who had his skin treated medically so that he could pass for a black, and what tremendous adjustments he had to undergo almost overnight.

But I am a member of a minority in many ways, and most of us are in some way. For one thing I represent a minority viewpoint in religion. I am a Unity student, and almost every Unity student, proud though he is to be one, is nevertheless often asked, "Is that the same as Christian Science?" or, "Is that the same as Unitarian?" or, "Do you people believe in Jesus Christ? Do you believe in the shed blood? Have you accepted Jesus Christ as your personal Savior?" To the first two I would say, "No, but we have some things in common." To the last three, "Yes, but possibly not in exactly the same way that you do." Most frequently, people do not even ask, but make their own often mistaken estimate of us by some chance contact with our publications, or even by reading tracts published by other minority religious groups who feel (and probably sincerely) that we are leading people astray.

Respectability

There isn't as much prejudice against us now as there used to be, in the beginning of Unity before and at the turn of the century. We are in fact becoming "respectable." The fact that many Unity congregations have prospered, obtained valuable properties, and built handsome churches has contributed to this. Better educational standards for our ministers has been a factor too. A growing number of clergymen in many denominations subscribe for Unity publications, even ask the prayers of Silent Unity, read Unity textbooks, and in some instances recommend these to members of their congregations.

Some of our ministers have served people high in government, in the realms of entertainment, the arts, and business, in matters of health, prosperity, or bereavement. Some of our ministers are prominent in fraternal orders, in civic projects, or have become popular in mass communication, such as radio, television, and the printed word. All these things have helped our "public image."

But I am not trying to justify people's approval of Unity so much as to offer some practical approaches as to how to meet the issue of just being a member of a minority, any minority. For in some degree at least we are all "minorities."

If you are left-handed, you are a member of a minority. So you may look a little odd—by which I mean simply different from most persons—in the way you handle knife and fork at the dining table. (You don't have to be different. You can learn to use eating implements the same as right-handers do it, if you want to enough).

You may look peculiar to some people as you sign a check with your left hand. But if the check is in their favor and is honored at the bank, they will accept it readily. Of if you are a baseball pitcher and can win more games than some of the right-handed ones, there will be no complaints except from the opposing teams.

Most people respect a job well done, and appreciate your help in time of need, regardless of whether you are a Catholic or a Jew or a Hottentot, or whether your skin is dark or fair, or whether you have a physical handicap and do not measure up to their notions of physical beauty.

In Emergencies

If your house is burning down, or your child needs artificial respiration, you will not be choosy about who comes to your aid.

So, if you are a member of a minority, what can you do to be more acceptable to other people, and hence happier and better adjusted? Because nobody lives to himself alone, however it may seem to be.

I asked a good friend of mine who from the majority viewpoint had several counts against him, how he meets the issue. This is what he told me:

"As you know, I am in a profession where almost every prominent member is a college graduate, and has one or more degrees. Financial pressure in an impoverished family and a physical handicap that I had to meet kept me from college. The only degrees I have are two honorary ones.

"In a time when every red-blooded American was expected to serve his country in the armed forces, I was rejected as 4-F.

"I tried to learn to speak in public and the first time I did so I got stage fright so bad that I had to rush off the platform and lose my breakfast, and then go back and finish the talk. (I knew that if I didn't, I'd never have the courage to try again).

"I got a job where I had to talk on the telephone a

170

great deal, and got so panicky over the technical terms of an unfamiliar business that my ears seemed to close up, and I couldn't hear. I quit the job and it took me months to prove to myself that it was *not my ears but my fears* that kept me from hearing.

"So what have I done? I think I have over-compensated to some degree.

"Some of the greatest men have had handicaps, and there's a theory that on occasion these have been blessings in disguise. Steinmetz was a hunchback. He withdrew from the world into a laboratory, where he outdid other scientists in discovery and invention. George Washington Carver was the son of Negro slaves. He devoted his energies to devising manifold uses for the basic product of the area where he was born—peanuts. He was offered many inducements to come North and work under more favorable conditions. Glenn Clark, who wrote his biography, brought him to worldwide attention, and quotes him as saying, 'No, the good Lord put me in the South and in the South I'll stay!' His dedication, his humility, and his service to others, black and white alike, made his name revered by millions. Edison was deaf, Beethoven was blind, Byron had a club foot, Charles Fillmore was a cripple.

"Me? I'm not a Steinmetz or a Carver or a Fillmore. But I've tried perhaps a little harder than most to excel in the things I do. I have deliberately taken on jobs that seemed beyond me and then tried to live up to them.

"I've cultivated people who knew more than I do about things that would enrich my life and thereby give me more to share with other people.

"I've tried for some attainments that have eluded

171

me, but I have had more opportunities offered me than I could have aspired to.

"I have hobnobbed with the humble and the great, and loved both equally. I've received more love and appreciation than any one man could expect from life.

"I'm still working hard. I'm still trying to improve my mind, I still read more books in a month than I am told the average person reads in a year. I still have an inferiority complex, but now I can grin over it. And since I am one-with-the-majority in this it helps to balance some of the other differences.

"How should we deal with minorities, racial, political, religious, or any other kind? I think we have to deal with them as individuals. The saying that putting men in uniform does not make uniform men has many applications. Putting men into categories doesn't make them the same either. And besides, people rise out of the categories that may have characterized them at some time. People, praise God, just will not stay in the pigeonholes in which dogmatists in religion or art, or just plain people, tend to put them.

"Now that I think of it, I don't much mind being in a minority.

"P.S. *I'm* left-handed, too."

The Love of Law
vs. the Law of Love

"You can make people hate you. You have to win their love," some wise person has said. In one way or another all of us are demonstrating this in daily living.

Lloyd C. Douglas tells the story of a young woman who passed on a legacy of bitterness to her young son that threatened to ruin his life and woefully affect the lives of people around him.

She had been badly mistreated and in her bitterness during her pregnancy as she lay in bed, she tore to bits the pages of a Testament with which someone had sought to console her. She brushed the fragments to the floor, and closed her eyes and wept.

She opened them to find her hand resting on one scrap of the printed page that had clung to the bedcovers. What she read on that fragment marked the beginning of a transformation in her own life, which was nearing its end. Troubled that she might have marked her unborn son, she wrote a letter to him and hid it in the secret drawer of a treasured desk. In his own young manhood, when he was rejected by his sweetheart, shunned by his fellows because of his morose bitterness, he came upon it, and read the story of how it came to be there: the story of her own self-destroying bitterness, and the message that changed her attitude. It read, *"Forgive us our trespasses, as we forgive those who trespass against us."*

Presumably the story was fiction, but it was true to fact, as much fiction is. Discussing this viewpoint with another author, an Englishman whose current novel impressed me as probably being the story of his own life, I ventured to ask, "Do you think that most authors write about their own experiences?"

He answered, "What else is there to write about?"

Many things, possibly, we might say, but none so convincing as those that come from our own heart.

Dr. Douglas, like most ministers, had a wealth of personal ministry and consultation to draw upon for book material. He knew what hollow comfort there is in bitterness, however justified; how little comfort in justice itself when it is love and mercy that we need.

Demand--or Invite?

The story of most people's lives is one of two things. Either they *demand* something of life or they *invite* something; they are either self-centered or people-centered. They are dominated either by a love of law, or by the law of love. The former are those who expect everybody to like them, cater to them, promote them, compensate them generously, because they feel that it is only just and right, that their self-appraised talents demand this.

The ruling theme of their life is justice, their own idea of justice, which is usually lenient toward themselves, exacting toward others. A man I once knew was of this type. He had worked very hard and over a long period of years to gain eminence in his profession as an actor, and even his competitors acknowledged his attainments. But the fact that he had never learned the difference between demanding his rights and inviting them, somehow seemed to keep him from receiving the full measure of acclaim his disciplined talents merited.

When a coveted role was in prospect, it seemed that if there was anyone else with equal or a little less proficiency available, the other man would be chosen. My friend would be chosen only from necessity and not from affection or preference. He had never learned the truth that *you can make people hate you, but you must win their love.* Sheer ability and justice are not really enough to fill the life of any of us with "that something" that all of us need for true fulfillment: a sense of being loved, approved, appreciated, not only for our attainments, but for ourself. It took my actor friend a lifetime to discover this, if indeed he ever really did. His pride was such that I could never broach the subject to him. I could only let him know by indirection that I saw his soul's need beneath his assumption of self-sufficiency. It was only near the end of his career that I could see that he was really mellowing, becoming more approachable, more outgoing, more appreciative of others and what they had to offer. As another friend of mine would say, "He just made the shade by sundown."

There are others who are almost the opposite, who seem to invite approval without seeking it; people who make you want to do things for them, who make you feel happy when something they do meets the approval of others, even above their approval of yourself.

After the Crash

A striking example of this kind of person is a woman whom I first came to know at a time when she and I and others were giving lecture-type book reviews of Douglas' first sensationally successful novel, "Magnificent Obsession." She was no longer young, except in

175

spirit. At the time I knew only that she and her husband had been affluent if not wealthy, that he had lost almost everything in the stockmarket crash of 1929, except a farm in Kansas, from which some of her old friends would persuade her to emerge and give a round of book reviews in churches and clubs. She told me some of her experiences over luncheon on such a visit.

"Were you, like the young woman in Douglas' novel, ever bitter?" I asked her.

"It was the fashion. Most of us young matrons whose husbands had been wiped out in the stock market were bitter. But I found bitterness, like self-pity, is a dead-end street. So I had to learn to adjust."

"Was there anything that specially helped you?"

"Well, yes, as a matter of fact, there was. Someone sent me a copy of a little booklet called *The Song of Life*. It was an interpretation of the Twenty-third Psalm. On the long lonely nights, when a prairie wind was howling about the eaves and my husband was restless, I'd read it over and over. It was my introduction to Unity, and probably saved my reason—that and a sense of humor."

A number of what I like to call mini-miracles seem to characterize my life pattern. The fact that I was the author of *The Song of Life*, and that this triggered a lifelong friendship and association, is certainly one of them.

At an End

At that point this woman seemed, at the age of fifty, to have come to an end of things. She had married young, reared three remarkable children in the affluence of her husband's apparently secure financial posi-

176

tion. Then along came the celebrated crash of 1929, bank failures, depression, during which some of her husband's associates jumped or fell from the windows of the exclusive club of which they were members.

All that remained to her and her husband was a rundown Kansas farm to which they retired, he into the retreat of bedridden illness, she to "learn to adjust" to the life of a farm woman, in contrast to the sophisticated urban social life that had occupied her life and energies until "the crash."

Such things as a drought, or the threat of a prairie fire, or even her husband's abrasive comments on her use of his shaving brush to whitewash the chicken coop, were diversions from the day-to-day round of chores.

Then came another blow. Her husband died.

By this time she was giving lecture-reviews at Unity, then teaching in the summer school. "I came in at the top," she once said smilingly.

"You might as well take the courses yourself," I suggested. And she did.

At the age of sixty, when many persons consider retiring, she started a new career, and became one of the outstanding women ministers of her era, interviewed on radio and television, author of magazine articles and a book, a sought-after speaker at religious and educational conventions, a women's-club favorite.

Her story (told here only in part, for it would make a book) is a graphic illustration of something that every spiritually aspiring person should know. There is a story in everybody's life.

"You can make people hate you; you have to win their love." The woman whom I knew at fifty and whose life was transformed at sixty, when she started a whole new career and became beloved of thousands, is an outstanding example of success by the law of love. She radiated enthusiasm. When you talked with her, she made you feel as if she would rather listen to you than anything else in the world. This spirit carried over into her ministry. She was ordained at sixty. When she talked about Bible characters to her class of hundreds, people would declare they could almost see the characters walking down the aisles.

This double law applies to people everywhere in every kind of situation. Another instance concerns a Hawaiian musician I came to know in a strange sort of way.

I happened to have a few days' vacation, made possible by pre-recording a daily television appearance to which I was committed. I flew to "one of my favorite places in all the world," as one television personality might put it. Friends invited me to a dinner dance at a famous hotel dining room. I dutifully but not too expertly piloted my hostess about the dance floor to the strains of a Hawaiian orchestra, when the young steel guitarist and tenor, whose artistry I had greatly admired on the screen, looked up as we passed by the bandstand, and said:

"Why, Dr. Wilson, what are you doing here?"

"I'm on vacation. How did you know my name?" I countered.

"I've watched you daily for almost a year. You've saved my life. May I come to your table when we have a break and tell you about it?"

And that's how I know that the law of love overcomes rivalry, jealousy, and alcoholism.

A Great Overcomer

He had, so he told me, an unhappy emotional experience. From the time he was five he had been an entertainer. Relatives swarmed about him like flies about a honeycomb. They not only milked him dry but in some cases added insult to injury. He resorted to drink. He became an alcoholic. He lost his job and his reputation. His fortunes were at low ebb when he happened to catch the brief Unity message it was my fortune to present on a daily variety program.

"I lived for those few minutes that would help me call upon the inner resources you talked about." His eyes were eloquent of love and gentleness as he talked. "I knew I had to forgive myself and forgive others so that I could clear the way for my good. This engagement marks my comeback. I might have expected taunts and ridicule from the other entertainers over the weakness I have shown—but I have never known such love."

"Only love could beget such love," I told him. "Cling to that. Don't let the old thoughts sneak back into your consciousness."

It was something over a year later that he and his wife had their first child, a boy. That the child is named for me makes me feel both humble and proud.

What prayer touched him most? Apparently the one of which I too am fond: *"The forgiving love of God has cleansed my life. Old thoughts and old things are as waters that have passed away. I forgive others as I would be forgiven. I claim my good and I press my claim. No man is against me and I am against no man. I am one with the omnipotent, omnipresent good."*

"A Number of Things"

Do you get a feeling sometimes as you are reading this book that some of the stories should be under a different chapter heading? I do, too, but none of them is all forgiveness, or all karma, or all thought power, or all love. They are all these things, with one attribute predominant at one time or in one approach to an experience, and quite another aspect of the inner life outstanding in another circumstance. After all, isn't that the way life really is?

In considering all these things, we must take care to avoid the pitfalls that entrap the thoughtless or arrogant nature that is still somewhere latent in anyone less than the embodied Christ; the tendency to pass judgment, to think with less than love and compassion upon those in whom we may have seen what appears to be a weakness which we would not indulge in ourself.

Turn with me to Matthew 5:21-22, which reads: "You have heard that it was said to the men of old, 'You shall not kill; and whoever kills shall be liable to judgment.' But I say to you that every one who is angry with his brother shall be liable to judgment; whoever insults his brother shall be liable to the council, and whoever says, 'You fool!' shall be liable to the hell of fire."

Don't Pass Judgment

No teacher worthy of the name will allow himself to be shocked by any confession given to him in confidence, nor will he pass judgment upon another's action or inaction. The counselor's one desire must be to help the one whose moment of weakness, confusion, or self-betrayal he may be privileged to share. Even in telling of personal experiences by which men and women have come into a better relationship to the law of love, it is in no sense to display human frailty, but rather to acclaim human ability to displace frailty by stalwart strength.

We are in effect all teachers, all students, all brothers, all overcomers. There is always the possibility that in viewing a moment of weakness in another person, we may be seeing that only; and may not have the greater privilege of seeing a hundred moments of the same person's strength and courage. We may observe that someone has yielded to a temptation, never knowing how many times he has withstood temptation.

We may allow ourself to be so enthralled by the love of law—even the law of action and reaction, cause and effect—that we fail to claim and acknowledge for others what we would plead for ourself, the law of love.

No one sees all of another person's life. We do not see all of our own. We are told that in the moment of peril, when the specter of death looms before us, our whole life passes in review before our mind's eye. I do not know if that is so. We can only hope and pray that in such a case, or in any case, what we call the good outweighs what we call evil. May it be so, and the creative forces of Being confirm what we believe; that evil always tends to destroy itself, until only the good endures; that

> "All things come right, and be it soon or late—
> All things come right at last to compensate
> For all the petty heartaches of today,
> For all the little failures on our way.
> For all our seeming sorrows, it appears,

181

Are really blessings in a mask of tears.
It is to test our courage, that is all,
And in the end each heart will seek its rest
Beside the one it always loved the best;
The darkest hour holds the brightest light,
And all things come right."

A Step Beyond

Most people will tell you, offhand, that they do not believe in such things as hunches, prophecies, fortune-telling, haunted houses, and similar "odd" things. Yet, introduce some such oddity from your own experience in a social gathering and before the evening is over virtually everyone will break down and admit (and apparently like to tell about) some such happening in his own life.

Why do people believe in such things?

Because they want to believe—although that is not the only reason.

Why they want to believe in such things may be more than wishful thinking. They may be responding to the ageless wisdom that seems to be innate in us all, the often deeply buried but innate "conviction of things not seen"; the dimly felt insistence that matter, the material world, the things we apprehend by the five senses, are not the sum of things but only a fraction (and a small one at that).

It is unwise to be too credulous about the odd experiences that may, just may, be evidential of *things beyond.* It is equally unwise to be too skeptical. "Now concerning spiritual gifts, brethren, I do not want you to be uninformed," said Paul, who went on to describe some of the very things we have mentioned. So the interest is not peculiar to, although heightened by the needs of, these times.

We used to be told that we should have nothing to do

with such things; either that they were fantasy and did not exist, or that they were the works of the devil. Such put-offs do not satisfy us any longer. We suspect that they *do* exist. It is a rash man who in these days will say that anything is impossible. Improbable, some of them, yes. Impossible, no. Modern man views the concept of a personalized devil, Satan, as being a naive shifting of responsibility for unpleasant happenings on some other shoulders than his own; at least, and somewhat frivolously, that "the devil, like Santa Claus, is your father in fancy dress."

Often it has seemed easier to deny the existence of things that are difficult—and on the basis of our present understanding and experience, impossible—to explain. But they do not go away. They keep reappearing.

Things Beyond

Are you one who as a child had invisible playmates?

Were they visitors from another dimension? Or, no matter how real they seemed, figments of your imagination? Inspired, possibly, by the fact that you may have been a lonely child who ingeniously took that means of fulfilling the heart's need for companionship? "I was a lonely child and never had any playmates, visible or invisible, at the time I needed them most," declares one unbelieving adult.

Have you found yourself thinking, in the midst of a conversation, "All this has happened before"? Or on a first visit to some place, have you seemed to know what lay beyond the hill? A reputable and very practically-minded businessman avows he had just such an experience. He was able to tell a scoffing friend who was with him that there would be a certain kind of house, with a white picket fence surrounding it, beyond a clump of trees; that they would see it when they topped the rise before them. And they did.

This kind of experience is described by psychologists and others as what the French call *déjà vu*, "already seen." My dictionary defines it: "A distortion of memory in which a new situation or experience is regarded as having happened before."

What Guided Him in the Temple?

A boy of twelve, now grown to manhood and become a very successful architect, had such a "distortion of memory" during a trip to Egypt. When they got to the Great Temple at Karnak he led the way ahead of the guide, describing to his mother what they would see next. There is apparently no easy explanation of such an occurence. The temptation is to say, "He must have been there in a pre-existence." That is a tenable theory, but there are other possible and simpler ones. He may have read about the temple (anticipating his later involvement in architecture). He may have read the thoughts of the guide who accompanied them, or of someone else who may have been entering the areas he and his mother were approaching. To dismiss the whole thing as chance does not seem quite reasonable.

"Such Stuff as Dreams"

Do you have dreams that seem to foretell later happenings in the waking state? J. W. Dunne, famous English mathematician, tells how he discovered that certain of his dreams bore a resemblance, either literal or figurative, to events that were to occur from two or three days to two or three weeks ahead. People whom I know describe similar dream-to-waking experiences.

However, do not most of your dreams, even the most impressive when you are dreaming them, or on occasion after you awaken, tend to shrink in significance when you relate them to another person? In doing so, you may find often against your desire that they are a dramatization or extension of something that happened a short while, maybe a day or two, before the dream.

Some persons relate experiences similar to Dunne's, but state that they occur not in sleep but in the time of reverie between waking and sleeping. They may seem to overhear conversations of which they are not a part, may observe persons and incidents with the kind of detachment that you feel, sitting in your car at the curb on a busy day, idly aware of persons coming and going to and fro. Into such reverie there will occasionally appear something that seems to foretell a real life happening. For any evidential value such an incident should be written down immediately after it is experienced, dated, sealed, and mailed to yourself or someone else. For in the waking state the will to believe often colors the dream to suit the reality.

Thought Transference

The case for telepathy is so well documented by this time that there are only a few cautionary comments to be made. One is that apparent thought transference, or extrasensory communication, most often happens between persons who are so familiar with each other's habits of thought, gesture, facial expressions that they can anticipate each other's reactions to a situation, or are likely to have the same thought about it simultaneously. Another is that such communications cannot be induced at will; and sometimes when it would be most helpful it does not come through.

Soul Memory?

Are there things you seem always to have known, never to have learned, or had occasion to learn in this life? One man asserts to having such an intuitive knowledge—he calls it "soul memory"—of certain forms of mystic symbolism: the symbolism of numbers, colors, geometrical figures, a theory of the fourth dimension, before ever having known that there was a considerable library of published works on such subjects. His discovery at the age of twenty of this latent knowledge within himself came about when he chanced upon a single issue of a defunct theosophical journal. In it was a casual reference to the symbolism of numbers. This seemed to trigger a response in him: "Why, I know about that!" He went to his typewriter and wrote down what "came to him" about several forms of symbolism, beginning with numbers. Later he ventured to share what he had written with some metaphysically oriented friends. They made him acquainted with books that confirmed his own spontaneous outpouring of ideas.

As curious as this, but more common, is the feeling we sometimes have that on a first meeting with someone, the stranger seems like an old friend returned after long absence. We accept him into our life without explanation or apology, as if we had always known him. Nor is the association always founded on a sense of friendship; it may actually be an area of hostility, or of obligation, a debt to be paid, a misunderstanding to be corrected.

The relationship takes on added importance to us, perhaps, or offers a reason for its existence, if we rationalize it as having carried over from a past life, and while it might be well not to rule this notion out entirely, it would be wiser perhaps to look for less mystical explanations. Often we find the answer in some resemblance to another person with whom we have had encounters in this life. An expression, a tone of voice, some mannerism, can set up a chain of mental and emotional reactions that give rise to a feeling of familiarity or even intimacy. It may go as quickly as it came, but there are instances where it has laid the foundation for a continuing and deepening relationship, varying from rapport to a sense of some unresolved duty or adjustment that must be settled.

A related phenomenon is revealed in visits, say to foreign countries. "On my first visit to London," a much-traveled friend tells me, "I had a profound sense of homecoming. Nothing seemed strange to me."

"You are a well-read man. You've probably read about it. Everybody who reads, goes to movies, watches television, knows about London."

"Yes," he answers a bit doubtfully, "but not what is around corners!"

I have to admit to the same feeling about London, and to a strongly adverse feeling about certain other places in Europe and the Orient.

We have "intimations" of something slightly beyond the senses, that mentally and emotionally may be compared to a thing seen out of the corner of the eye, as we say. We may feel convinced that what we have experienced is strongly evidential or even proof of some form of extrasensory perception; immortality or reincarnation.

Life beyond This

Have you had intimations of life after death?

Most of us do not think very much about death in the early years of our life. It is something that happens to other and older people, and occasionally to other young people. That sooner or later it happens to everyone is a shadowy intimation that we hope will go away if only we ignore it. Sometimes something happens that seems like an intrusion from another world, as if just maybe, perhaps, there is a return in some degree of a person who has died, or as we say euphemistically, has "passed on."

Something of this happened in my family when I was about fifteen. A member of the family apparently went into a trancelike state, and purported to bring a "message" from my grandmother. The experience was eerie and frightened me. I was asked not to be alarmed, to be quiet, and it would be explained to me later. It appeared that from time to time through the years something similar had occured. Other members of the family considered it a kind of disgrace, like a moral transgression, and a promise had been exacted from my mother that she would not let me know about this peculiar gift or affliction.

That there might be other explanations for the phenomenon, as something originating not in the afterlife but in the subconscious of the medium, was something that only after many months I was to contemplate. The experience was unsettling, but it served to introduce me to a world of thought, speculation, experimentation, and surmise that I had not known existed.

I found that there were reputable people, people of erudition and probity, who took such matters seriously; who were interested not only in intimations of immortality, but were intent upon knowing more about the intricate workings of the extensions of the human personality, the nature of the subconscious and superconscious, whatever these might signify, and wherever they might lead.

As time went on I became more and more skeptical, or at least much less impulsive, about accepting "proof" of immortality based upon extrasensory perception. But at the same time I discovered in myself a growing conviction of the reasonableness of the continuity of life.

I could no longer seriously entertain the religious concept presented to me in the established church, that man's entire future throughout eternity should be dependent upon his adherence to or deviation from a plan of salvation loosely related to the Holy Scriptures.

I could no longer believe that the simple release from the human body would make us either angels or devils, consigned to heavenly bliss or hellish torture forever.

It seemed to me that if immortality is a fact in the natural (or should I say supernatural) experience of mankind, then what we call death would simply be birth viewed from the underside—death as related to this plane of life, birth as related to a higher, or at least a physically intangible realm. Just as when we awaken in the morning after a night's sleep we are the same person we were when we went to bed, and we go on from where we left off the day before, so in death we awaken as from a sleep and go on from where we left off.

Conclusive proof of life after death is hard to come by, not because there is lack of evidence, but because it is difficult to come upon evidence that makes any other explanation impossible.

The will to believe is very strong. The ability to become completely objective is difficult to attain. And whatever we experience is reality seen from a certain level of awareness and a location in time and space. Where you stand determines what might be called your "line of sight."

Many evidential experiences have come to me personally and to persons well-known to me. I have read about hundreds of others in scores of books dealing with this subject.

The Missing Will

One of the most striking experiences I know about involved a woman who was a successful practicing osteopathic physician until her recent demise. I have told the story in an earlier book of mine, now out of print. She had received her training in Kirksville, Missouri under Dr. Andrew Taylor Still, founder of osteopathy. Her practice was, and had been for many years, in Los Angeles, where I knew her. She was proud of her profession and training, a woman of naturally cautious and careful thought, confirmed by her many years of medical practice.

She had gone to Boston to attend a medical convention, and while there had looked up a long-time friend, a woman who had recently been bereaved by the death of her husband.

The woman's appearance was tragic. She confessed

191

that it was not only the death of her husband that troubled her, but that contrary to his usual meticulous habits, he had failed to keep a promise, the promise to change his will. The results of this were proving disastrous to the family fortunes, which were under the control of her son, a young man who was recklessly extravagant and emotionally unstable. Disaster threatened unless this erratic behavior could be curbed.

Her husband had made a will during the son's boyhood, enabling him to have charge of the family fortune, which at the time had seemed to both parents a means of freeing the boy's mother of responsibility in her later years. As he grew to manhood and they observed signs of instability in the youth's nature, they had discussed the advisability of making a new will. This her husband promised to do. His wife thought no more about the matter since he was scrupulous about keeping promises. However, following his demise, no new will could be found, and the estate was administered under the provisions of the one that had been under discussion.

So the situation remained when my doctor friend returned to California. Shortly after her return she received an unexpected phone call. It was from a woman completely unknown to her.

"Do you know anyone by the name of So-and-so?" she asked. The name she used was that of the doctor's Boston friend.

Assured that she did, the woman told a remarkable story. She gave her name, and stated that she was staying at the Gates Hotel in downtown Los Angeles. "You wouldn't know me," she explained, "and it seemed

192

very silly even to call you until you told me you recognized the name I mentioned. I have been fooling around with a ouija board and it began to spell out a message. It was supposed to be from a man whose wife lives in Boston. He said he was troubled because his wife thought he had failed to keep a promise about a paper of some kind.

"He gave me your name, which is an unusual one, and I would have dismissed the whole thing if I had not found your name just as he gave it, listed in the telephone directory. That made me think it might be true. He asked me to try to reach you and relay a message; he had put the paper she was concerned about between the pages of a volume of Shakespeare's plays in the family library."

The doctor went immediately to the phone and called her widowed friend, to give her the message.

"Hold the line while I look," she exclaimed.

She returned to the phone a few moments later to report that the will was indeed hidden between the pages of the volume indicated in the message . . . a message conveyed by a woman unknown to anyone involved. (It just occurs to me to wonder whether any acknowledgment was ever made to the unknown woman at the Gates!)

Here is an instance of apparent "communication" that comes as near satisfying what are sometimes called "test conditions" as any I know of:

The location of the will was unknown to any living person.

The channel through whom the message came was unknown to anyone concerned.

The persons, even their names, were unknown to the woman at the Gates.

Intimations

Taken at face value, this incident offers as definite a case for communication with the Beyond as I know; more evidential than most accounts that have appeared in books dealing primarily with this subject. It is the kind of incident that is difficult for seriously thinking people to brush aside. Maybe we will have to extend research in ESP before we will know exactly what it signifies. There may be some other explanation than the most obvious one for this and kindred other-worldly episodes. We are beginning to discover potentials within the subconscious of the individual that are amazing.

It is conjectured that there are a few persons who can bring up from the subconscious knowledge that transcends that of the conscious mind: that such persons may even tap what might be called the universal subconscious, which may be another name for what is called the Akashic Records, the total wisdom of the Creative Forces. In principle we all have access to this fount of knowledge. The proper approach to it, according to the great teachers, is in prayer and meditation.

"Except Ye Become . . ."

What did Jesus mean when He said, "Truly, I say to you, unless you turn and become like children, you will never enter the kingdom of heaven"?

There are many things about little children that touch the heart, many things perhaps that it would be desirable for us to emulate: their simplicity, their freedom from calculating guile, their frankness, their touching faith in us older ones. But more than any of these is something I look for in the eyes of the very young. It was first brought to my attention, oddly enough, by a painting—the portrayal of a contemporary mother, holding a little boy in her lap. A copy of the painting, by Jessie Wilcox Smith, hung on my study wall. Sometimes I would stand and study it, and marvel that the artist could have caught on canvas the look of wide-eyed wonder she so marvellously portrayed. To my own gaze it seemed as if his eyes looked not only at me but beyond me, not only in space but in time. For his mother seemed to be Mary, he the infant Jesus. Was this in the mind of the artist? Was she thinking as she painted that He was looking down the years to His destiny, the calling of the Twelve, the Last Supper, the Transfiguration, the Garden, Golgotha, the Resurrection?

Wonder looks out through those bright little-boy eyes, and I think it may be this attribute of childhood wonder that Jesus was alluding to when He said, "Unless you turn and become like children, you will never enter the kingdom of heaven." Without disloyalty to His meaning, then, we might paraphrase the passage to read, "Unless you regain the sense of wonder you had as children, you will never enter the kingdom."

Childhood Wonders

Can you remember when you were a little child, your own feeling of wonder as you discovered texture and color and moving things, people, worms and grass and mud and butterflies and birds and sky, and loving arms that held you close, voices that crooned a lullaby?

Can you remember believing in Easter eggs and Easter bunnies and Santa Claus and skyrockets that circled the moon, long before anyone but little children could really believe it possible? Or that storks indeed brought babies and dropped them down sooty chimneys without their getting so much as a smudge of soot upon them?

Did you have playmates that apparently grownups could not see—but for the very good reason that these little friends always disappeared when grownups came upon the scene?

Something went out of our life when we had to face the debunking of these denizens of our childhood world. Nor has our grownup world been exempt from the same denigration of the greats of our own mores, by which we have tended largely to debunk the legendary exploits of national heroes, and to celebrate the anti-heroes of our time instead.

Even the religious world has not been exempt from these inroads. (I suppose I shall never forget my feelings when I first learned about the so-called "higher criticism," which would have us believe that Jesus Christ

196

never lived except in the imagination of bigots. I thought I must find Him for myself or else in all honesty renounce my calling. I think I know how Mary felt when she cried, "They have taken away my Lord, and I do not know where they have laid him.")

Keeping the Faith

A businessman who has long been a student of Unity returned to his church in Kansas City recently, and recalled the thrill and excitement and sense of purpose that were stirred by the project of financing, planning, building what might be called the Mother Church.

"Do you still have that enthusiasm about your faith that carried us all through that exciting time? Don't ever lose it. It is what keeps people young and growing.

"For some time now I've been active in a church which has in the past few years outgrown its facilities. We have more than a hundred thousand dollars in the treasury, which would enable us to buy adjoining property on which to extend our present building, but the Board will not let go of it. Can you guess why? They say if they spent all that money for the land, there wouldn't be any money left for the building. I asked them how much money the organization had when the original church was built. They said, 'None.'

"All right, then, let's give the money away to some worthy cause, and start from scratch. You had enough faith to do it then. Let's see how much faith we have to do it again!"

"If I were part of a building program today," says a prominent minister, "I would never let the building be completely finished. I'd plan it so that there would always be some prominent windows with factory glass, awaiting the time when they could be transformed by the iridescent colors of stained glass. I'd let the structural concrete stand out mutely on a wall that needed carved and panelled wood to delight the eye. Too often when a big building is finished, the people's enthusiasm gradually wanes. They are content to sit back, and at first admire and recall, then take for granted and become oblivious to the project that for a time so inspired them. They are likely to take religious truth, their minister too, for granted. They sometimes make me feel as if they are practically defying me to tell them something they do not know! They have lost the vision of the truth that it is not what you know, but what you do about what you know, that counts. When you stop doing, you stop vitally living, and tend merely to exist. In an organization this is dead wood. It is stultifying."

The same thing applies to ministers as to members of their flock. There was one such minister who in his young manhood experienced what was called a miracle healing of Pott's disease. It led him into the ministry, and for a time his work attracted a following of those who were impressed by his story. But people do not become more and more impressed, usually, by hearing the same story over and over. Instead of his healing being an incentive to greater expansion of his own faith, which might have kindled faith within others, it seemed to make him feel that he had arrived; and after you have arrived, where is there to go? He did no mighty works from then on.

There is no new truth. Truth is a constant. Our discoveries of its manifold aspects and applications are ever new, often exciting. The possibilities of radio, of television, of flights into outer space have always existed, awaiting man's discovery. More inventions and discoveries have been made in the past fifty years than in all previous known history, so we are told.

Part of the reason for so much unrest, violence, and rejection of "the establishment" can be attributed to the possibility that we have not learned to adjust mentally and emotionally to the rapid pace of material progress. The last frontier of discovery may very well be that of inner space, a quieter and less easily recognized form of progress that is under way.

We have gained much in worldly knowledge, in material progress, in sophistication in this incredible twentieth century—but in our pursuit of "the new" we have lost something beyond price: the sense of faith, of wonder.

Faith does not negate intellectual attainment. It *fulfills* all worldly wisdom. But intellect cannot heal a broken body. It does not bring content and peace of mind. It cannot comfort the broken-hearted. It offers no human breast to lean upon, no warm enfolding arms, no heartening voice to murmur, "I understand," or to affirm, "I know you can make it," when despair overwhelms you.

Seek, Find, Regain

Seek out the young (if there are none readily at hand) that you may discover that look of wonder in their eyes, and by association find help in recapturing your own lost sense of wonder. Remember, though, that in these days of television they must be very young indeed! When you find them, go on a trip with them into the magic kingdom where it is Christmas every day of the year, and sometimes the Fourth of July. On this trip you'll need no drug except remembering.

Reach past thought to feeling, because it is in feeling that healing, joy, forgiveness, and sweet assurance dwell. In doing so you may recapture the long-lost rapture of the kingdom in which all things good are possible, and only the good is enduringly true.

Can you regain that which was lost? Yes, if you will remember that feeling is as legitimate a posture of maturity as is intellect. And feeling is the secret.

Contemplation

Practice contemplative thought. I once had marginal contact with a famous actress who has spanned fifty years and more on stage and screen. She has changed but little in appearance from the days of D. W. Griffith and other giants of the silent screen. She was observed one day on the set of a later period between "takes," while boom mikes and cameras were being moved about, with directors and prop men rushing here and there, make-up artists and wardrobe people bustling about. Seated in one of the familiar canvas chairs, she was lost in quiet contemplation of a single rose, oblivious to the hubbub of activity about her, lost in a world of her own.

I found that she seemed to sustain that atmosphere off the set as well. She had regained (or perhaps sustained) that sense of wonder that lifts us into the sense of serene dominion that Jesus may have been alluding to when He said we must become as children.

The world is full of wonders. We should not let ourself lose sight of them. The world of asphalt and concrete and high-rise buildings and problems of air and earth and water pollution may partially conceal them from us, although many of man's creations are full of wonders too. Take time to look, really look, at a sunrise or sunset, or the sky when a storm is brewing. Find some calm expanse of water and go and sit by it, seek out a gurgling stream and listen to its music. Lift up your eyes to the hills, or from the hills look down to the valley below. "The heavens are telling the glory of God; and the firmament proclaims his handiwork."

Another Way

There is another way into the world of wonder too—a very personal way. It is simple and quiet. It may seem so habitual that you have taken it for granted. It is your experience of things that are not quite of this outer realm even though they take place in it. You may be shopping. Suddenly you have the impulse to make a turn, and thereby run into a friend you had longed to see. Or you may have the urge to phone or write to someone you have not contacted for a while, and are greeted by the response, "How did you know that I needed a word from you right now?" Or your own phone rings, and you answer it to find the person of whom you have been thinking is calling you. Or with no prompting on your part someone gives you a book you wanted; or you try to think of a quotation you want to use, and are "led," as we say, to the book that includes it; or you seek a Bible passage and open to the very page on which it appears.

Important? Significant? Who can say, except that in the experience of them you find a sense of a sustaining, reassuring Presence that puts you in tune, that makes you feel stronger, more capable, more at peace with

201

yourself and the world around you. You acknowledge a world of wonder. It gives life to an affirmation that you probably have known as words, which you can now repeat with a deeper sense of meaning: *I am now in the presence of pure being, and immersed in the holy spirit of life, love, and wisdom.*